THE TH
WIT

Power, Love and Wisdom
in the Garden of the Gods

CHRISTOPHER
PENCZAK

COPPER
CAULDRON
PUBLISHING

Acknowledgments

A special thanks to many amazing people without whom this book would not be possible—to my partners, Steve Kenson and Adam Sartwell, for all your support, love, and guidance; to my parents, Ronald and Rosalie, for the unending support and encouragement; and to all the people who have offered support with this book, including Copper Cauldron, the Temple of Witchcraft, Derek Yesman, Andrea Neff, Lisa Dubbels, Sandi Liss, Stephanie Taylor, Raven Grimassi, Dorothy Morrison, Ellen Dugan, Joe and Doug of Otherworld Apothecary, David Rankine, Sorita D'Este, and Sa Hu-Sia-Heka.

Credits

Editing: Andrea Neff
Cover Design: Derek Yesman
Interior Art: Derek O'Sullivan (Figure 6), Christopher Penczak
Layout: Adam Jury
Publisher: Steve Kenson

For more information, visit:
www.christopherpenczak.com
www.coppercauldronpublishing.com

First Printing

Printed in the USA.

Praise for the Three Rays:

"Christopher Penczak has done it again: The Three Rays of Witchcraft is simply amazing. Whether one is just starting to explore the world of witchcraft or has been around the block a few times doesn't matter – there is something here for everyone. Christopher presents unique and compelling concepts in a wonderfully intelligent manner. But wait there's more – unlike many other pagan authors Christopher does his homework. There is more solid information in the Introduction alone than in the sum total of other books on the subject. The Three Rays of Witchcraft is a must have for any serious occult library."

— Jimahl Di Fiosa, Alexandrian High Priest and author of *A Voice in the Forest* and *Talk to Me*

"Christopher Penczak has drawn together material from diverse pagan roots and magical sources, blended in the cauldron of his own experience and shaped by the light of his vision and inspiration to present a coherent and vibrant system of practice. The theology of his work is syncretic and inclusive, opening the gates of the three worlds and inviting the reader to walk the paths of power, love and wisdom and find their own way. It is an offering full of angels and fairies, gods and humans, diverse yet connected and each with their own powers and wisdom. This book has strength in its mutability, presenting practical material that is easily adapted, and it will surely be one of the most enchanting flowers in the Garden of the Gods."

— Sorita d'Este, Author of *Hekate Liminal Rites, Practical Planetary Magick, The Guises of the Morrigan* and founder of Avalonia Books.

Other books by Christopher Penczak

City Magick (Samuel Weiser, 2001)

Spirit Allies (Samuel Weiser, 2002)

The Inner Temple of Witchcraft (Llewellyn Publications, 2002)

The Inner Temple of Witchcraft CD Companion (Llewellyn Publications, 2002)

Gay Witchcraft (Samuel Weiser, 2003)

The Outer Temple of Witchcraft (Llewellyn Publications, 2004)

The Outer Temple of Witchcraft CD Companion (Llewellyn Publications, 2004)

The Witch's Shield (Llewellyn Publications 2004)

Magick of Reiki (Llewellyn Publications 2004)

Sons of the Goddess (Llewellyn Publications 2005)

The Temple of Shamanic Witchcraft (Llewellyn Publications 2005)

The Temple of Shamanic Witchcraft CD Companion (Llewellyn Publications 2005)

Instant Magick (Llewellyn Publications 2005)

The Mystic Foundation (Llewellyn Publications 2006)

Ascension Magick (Llewellyn Publications 2007)

The Temple of High Witchcraft (Llewellyn Publications 2007)

The Temple of High Witchcraft CD Companion (Llewellyn Publications 2007)

The Living Temple of Witchcraft Volume I (Llewellyn Publications 2008)

The Living Temple of Witchcraft Volume I CD Companion
(Llewellyn Publications 2008)

The Living Temple of Witchcraft Volume II (Llewellyn Publications 2009)

The Living Temple of Witchcraft Volume II CD Companion
(Llewellyn Publications 2009)

The Witch's Coin (Llewellyn Publications, 2009)

Contents

Exercises

Charts

Figures

INTRODUCTION

One of the most challenging things about modern Witchcraft is reconciling the theology, or lack of clear theology, we have inherited. Today, Witchcraft is a collection of a wide range of practices, a religion incorporating folklore and mythology from all around the globe. Our spiritual practice involves diverse rituals and symbols, and unconsciously adopts conflicting views on divinity and the world. While diversity is great, the lack of cohesion between our symbols and cultures can create misunderstandings and prevent us from having a clear worldview rooted in the modern Witch's understanding of the universe and how we relate to it. This problem of theology can be so difficult that many Witches don't attempt to resolve the holes in our worldview. Like the proverbial elephant in the room, the issues of our mismatched practices loom so large that many of us can't see them. We don't understand the need our spirit, mind, and heart have to reconcile all the parts of our experience and learning, so we don't attempt to synthesize something new from all the parts.

Modern Witches have inherited a cornucopia of lore, myths, and traditions. Some of us have been handed this horn of plenty from teachers, groups, and books. Others have received a half-empty horn, a spilled cup, and learned how to fill it themselves. Yet we seek a tradition that is not a grouping of disparate parts, but something that is a cohesive whole. When we empty out our horn and try to make a stew with all the ingredients, when we really look them over, we find many flavors that don't work well together in the standard recipes we know. Our many parts don't fit. They don't blend together. That stark realization leaves us with several choices.

We can choose to keep these pieces separate, a collection of individual parts that will serve us individually but not nourish us as a whole. While that is a viable option—and we can even separate the pieces into groups from specific cultures and lands and use them only in traditional "recipes" of religious thought from those lands—we might not have all the other necessary ingredients. We don't live in those cultures, times, and places. Moreover, this separation seems to go against our desire to reconcile all we've learned, as well as our basic curiosity and desire to experiment.

We also can choose to use all the conflicting ingredients and make something unpalatable. While this would make use of all the ingredients at hand, would anybody want to "eat" it? Probably not, though many would simply to deny they had made a bad choice, and thus swallow an unpalatable blend in pride. Experimentation does generate its share of mistakes, and we shouldn't be so proud that we can't admit that.

Or we can work with what we have—changing some ingredients with a bit of work, discarding others that don't quite fit our needs—and create a new recipe based on the knowledge and respect of the past recipes yet with a new twist appropriate for us in the modern age. We can reconcile the parts and synthesize a new way that pays homage to the old, that is rooted in many lands, yet is unique to the time and place in which we now live. That is the path I have chosen in the Craft.

The lore we have inherited is not always particularly cohesive, and in our further studies, to expand our understanding of the art, we gather more bits and pieces to add to the incoherence. We continue to put more and more ingredients in our horn, but we still don't know what do with them. Another, less palatable image of what goes on in the quest of modern Witches is what I call "magpie syndrome." We tend to collect the bright and shiny. We are attracted to new and pretty things, and we hoard them but never really put them to use. We never really make anything out of them. Instead, we should let our new lore rot a bit, let it mix and mingle with earth and create a fertile ground. From such soil the strongest new trees will grow.

The "motherland" of modern Witchcraft, the British Isles, was a great melting pot of ideas, philosophies, and religions during the time of the Witchcraft Renaissance. Starting in the late eighteen hundreds through the mid twentieth century, when Gerald Gardner first went public with his Craft, now known as Gardnerian Wicca, a wide array of occult ideas were planted and grew roots. Yet one can question how deep some of them went in history and how fertile was the ground in which they were planted. For good or ill, this tradition has become the platform for modern Witches, and even in this day of great criticism of Gardner, he has done us a great service by initiating the growth of modern Witchcraft in a way that has become accessible to us.

Late-nineteenth-century Britain gave rise to the Hermetic Order of the Golden Dawn, arguably one of the most influential Western magickal traditions of the modern era. With a background in Freemasonry and Rosicrucian study, the founders of the Golden Dawn brought together the teachings of Jewish Qabalah, Christian mysticism, Egyptian religion, Greek philosophy, Hindu mysticism, Hermeticism, Renaissance grimoires, alchemy, Enochian angel magick, tarot, and psychic development under the cohesive banner of the Tree of Life.

Though technically born even earlier in the United States, Theosophy, the brainchild of Madame Blavatsky, influenced the occultists of Britain considerably. Eastern mysticism was taking a foothold in both Britain and the United States, filling a spiritual void that modern Western religions were not addressing. Blavatsky brilliantly seized upon some of these themes and fused the Hindu and Buddhist currents with Greek, Egyptian, and Persian concepts, without necessarily denying the mysticism of Christianity though not directly focusing on it. Her spiritual inheritor (if not the direct personal "inheritor" of the Theosophical movement), Alice Bailey, emphasized the Christian element but added greatly to the science of Theosophical thought through psychology, astrology, the seven rays, and "white" magick.

William W. Westcott, a founder of the Golden Dawn, was apparently a Theosophist as well, and brought his understanding of Theosophy to the formation of the Golden Dawn. Dion Fortune, though not a Witch herself, greatly influenced the modern Wicca movement, particularly through her novels *The Sea Priestess* and *Moon Magic*. She was both a Theosophist and a magician of the Golden Dawn, and went on to found her own movement, eventually renamed the Society of the Inner Light. In her writings, she outlined a theology of the rays, which has particularly influenced me, as her focus was on the three rays of Power, Wisdom, and Love. Fortune described these three rays as the impetus for three emigrations of magickal practitioners from Atlantis out into the world. Both the Golden Dawn and Theosophy were influenced by the earlier, growing Spiritualist movement, which popularized mediumship and greatly influenced seekers in both the United States and Britain.

During the eighteenth century, the United Kingdom enjoyed a Druidic revival, with various colorful characters espousing a very romantic notion of ancient Druidism and how it could be reclaimed by modern people. Here we have the first notions of the stately priestlike Archdruid holding ceremony at Stonehenge, whereas the historical Druids more likely were shamanic and often skin wearers rather than the stately court magicians that people imagine when they think of Druids today. Though most of eighteenth-century Druidism was based on imagination and flights of fancy, the first Druidic Revival did renew an interest in a Native British tradition and influenced the occultists to come, even sowing the seeds of our own modern Druidic traditions.

The legacy of these traditions was the birthing ground for the Witchcraft revival. By the time Gardner went public with his tradition of Witchcraft, all this information not only was available to him but was part of the culture of occultism at the time. He used this esoteric legacy, along with the sometimes controversial works of Margaret Murray, Robert Graves, and Sir James George Frazer. At the time, the common folk image of the strange man or woman involved in the esoteric was a Witch, regardless of whether the individual was practicing a form of native pagan religion or folk magick. If a person was a medium, Theosophist, magician, or other kind of occultist, it was easy to be mistaken for a Witch.

Such individuals, few and far between compared to today, did manage to network despite the lack of modern conveniences, such as computers or the

Internet. Gardner, working to revive the religion of Witchcraft from the fragments he inherited from his New Forrest Coven, also was involved in Freemasonry, ceremonial magick, the Druidic revival, and Eastern studies. He even had contact with Aleister Crowley, a controversial former member of the Golden Dawn, and was offered a charter to Crowley's organization, the O.T.O., or Ordo Templi Orientis.

After Gardner came the reign of the "King of the Witches," Alex Sanders, who was even better at achieving notoriety than Gardner. Sanders' Witchcraft emphasized a ceremonial flair in harmony with the Golden Dawn teachings. The two men started the most influential lines of modern Witchcraft, known today as British Traditional Wicca, or the Gardnerian line and the Alexandrian line.

Since these two men went public as Witches, a variety of other Witchcraft traditions have come about, each adding something to the mix. The Feminist movement added a spiritual dimension with an emphasis on Goddess reverence, and many took the rites and rituals of Witchcraft to create Goddess-focused Feminist traditions. Resurgent interest in Native American traditions led to the addition of popular "shamanic" techniques and worldview to the modern Craft. There is even some evidence that Native American traditions were imported into England through youth groups and possibly influenced Gardner's rituals. Many seeking a more primal form of spiritualism explored African diasporic traditions, with their unbroken links to African native religions, and then added such practices to the Craft. Laurie Cabot added insight from modern quantum physics to focus on "Witchcraft as a science." Some Witches, conflicted over their Christian upbringing and pagan leanings, sought to reconcile the two in Christian Wicca, or an exploration of the Arthurian mythos. Dion Fortune was a strong advocate of the blend of British paganism and Christianity found in the Arthurian myth cycle. Many modern Witches are interested in holistic health, and have been drawing from a variety of Eastern lore from China, Japan, and India. This "magpie-ing" has filled our collective cornucopia, yet we are unsure what to do with the knowledge.

My own practice has brought me from the realms of Witchcraft to the shamanism of the Americas and Siberia, to Celtic Reconstructionism, to herbalism and flower essences, to Reiki energy healing and Eastern medicine, to Hinduism, and to channeling, crystals, and Theosophy by way of the modern ascension movement. I've collected a lot of tools, but Witchcraft has always been my toolbox. Witchcraft is the lens through which I look at the world.

I struggle to reconcile my own personal practice within the framework of Witchcraft. Sometimes my practice works and sometimes it does not, yet the Craft has been my grounding and framework, encouraging me and allowing me to absorb new information and skills, putting them to immediate use and synthesizing something new where my peers without the Witchcraft background often flounder and forget the tools they already have.

Still, all of these tools and techniques draw from different cultures, worldviews, and theologies. Polytheistic, monotheistic, pagan, animistic, pantheistic, transcendental, panentheistic, Indo-European, ecstatic, stoic, and Gnostic are just a few of the words used to describe them. These ideas are not necessarily complementary, as they often are rooted in conflicting worldviews. While there may be a shared core truth found in all mystical religions, it is not in all religions, and even the mystical ones get you to that core truth by very different routes. The worldview of the ancient pagan is very different from that of the modern Christian, no matter how you look it. Eastern perspectives on life are very different from Western ones. The ideas of nature-based traditions are different than those with a different root. And the worldview of the modern Witch is still not clear. We are in the first steps of a new way that is rooted in the Old Ways and pays homage to the past, yet we cannot ignore what has come since the supposed Golden Ages when our spiritual ancestors flourished. The reconciliation process involves finding which tools fit your toolbox and support your worldview and magickal spirituality. Those that are abhorrent to your worldview have to be either discarded or transformed. My catalyst for transformation actually came from advocates for the past, for the more traditional ways over the modern ones.

One of the treasures from the time of Gerald Gardner—which is only just reaching the popular consciousness of the "mainstream" Witchcraft community—is now popularly known as Traditional Craft. The term is used to distinguish it from what is seen as the modern movement of Wicca, both the formal lineage-based British Traditional Wicca and the modern eclectic self-initiated Wicca. Practitioners of Traditional Craft claim a pre-Gardnerian root that has developed separately from the overall modern Witchcraft movement, though some are admitting they obviously have been influenced by the pagan movement, and some are now using the term Modern Traditional Witchcraft to be both accurate and distinct.

One of Gardner's most fervent critics is in many ways considered the most public proponent of this type of Craft. Known as Robert Cochrane, but born as Roy Bowers, this gentleman is credited with creating the term Gardnerian as a derogatory slur for those Witches trained by Gardner, as Cochrane did not consider them real Witches. Though Cochrane never wrote any books, and died at the age of thirty-five from an overdose of belladonna—possibly an act of suicide—we know him from writings and a series of letters he wrote to a series of people, including an American seeker named Joe Wilson and British ceremonial magician Willian Gray. He also communicated with Doreen Valiente, Gardner's High Priestess, who later left Gardner to work with Chochrane and then left Cochrane, equally disenchanted. Cochrane's lore has been a subtle but strong influence on modern Witches of every tradition. His letters have circulated via photocopies and now on the Internet, until they were finally bound into a book simply called *The Robert Cochrane Letters*. The influence of his ethos, and of traditions like his, is rising in the Witchcraft communities. Authors such as Andrew Chumbley, Daniel Schulke, Nigel Jackson, Nigel Pennick, Robin Artisson, and Orion Foxwood continue in this vein and expose different lines of Traditional Craft.

I have connected with practitioners who claim a line from Cochrane's tree, branching out before Cochrane and his Clan on Tubal Cain were ever known. Without betraying oaths on either side, we discussed philosophies and theologies, from the Traditional Witch view of their Craft to the thoroughly modern one of mine. I was honored to participate in a ritual with them and be introduced to others in this quiet yet growing movement in our subculture. It was through this contact that I first heard of their teaching of the bent line, the straight line, and the crooked line, now popularized through a podcast called *The Crooked Path* by Traditional Witch, author, and publisher Peter Paddon.

Though for some it would be tempting to simply seek out this tradition and perhaps a more cohesive and authentic lineage to the past, that has never been my way. In the new aeon, I believe we all are challenged to create new forms with respect to the old, but our practice must evolve. Some of us will be charged with keeping the lines of wisdom and culture separate and evolving on their own. Others will be charged with authentically reconstructing the past based on scholarship and poetic insight. Still others are called to weave all of these lines into a new tapestry of wisdom. I feel a kinship with this third group, in the spirit of Theosophy, the Golden Dawn, and Doreen Valiente.

While in meditation, the concept of the three lines came to me spontaneously, striking me with a vision. This vision congealed my understanding of three, as the concept of three forces, three ways, or even three rays as found in the many traditions I have studied. Mimicking the modern Druidic image of *awen*, or inspiration, I saw three dots, the three drops from the Cauldron of Inspiration. Emanating from those three drops I saw three rays. Traditionally they are drawn as three straight lines, but not so in my vision.

The first ray, on the left, was straight like a spear, ending in a pointed tip. The second ray, on the right, was curved and bent like a branch, with three flowers, one four-petalled, one five-petalled, and one six-petalled. The third ray, in the center, was a crooked serpent with ram horns and a forked tongue. The entire image was encircled by three rings. In that moment, I reconciled in an entirely new way my understanding of the powers of Witchcraft, ceremonial magick, Druidism, shamanism, and Theosophy. All the fragments came together, transformed into a wonderful new brew. When I awoke from the vision, I feverishly wrote down all the insights I was having, and the result became the basis of several workshops and rituals. Upon further experimentation, meditation, and consideration of the insights of others, you have the final result in your hands, though I'm sure this modern grimoire is but a first step, and our understanding of the three rays of Witchcraft will evolve and unfold with time and magick.

At this turn of the ages, as we seemingly enter a new aeon of spiritual evolution, I have said that it is the job of some practitioners to keep the threads of cultures and traditions clearly separate, so they may develop on their own. This is the job of the traditionalists and reconstructionists: preserving each strand. The job of other practitioners is to synthesize, weaving many strands together into a harmonious whole. These are the innovators, experimenters, and edge walkers. I personally have chosen the latter, not only because of my personal preference but in the fervent belief that at this time such work is needed. While I value each of the individual cultures and traditions that I draw upon, global consciousness is the hallmark of our new age, where we must find a global identity and shared purpose as the people of Earth. We must expand our concept of tribalism to include all people and all lands to step into this new age, while preserving, sharing, and celebrating our differences. I believe that each culture and religion has developed a part of the whole for the new age, yet each is incomplete on its own, like having a piece of a mosaic but not the whole picture. We often assume our piece is the only piece that matters, ignoring the influence of all others. Now is the time to bring those pieces together, to create not just one collective vision but many patterns where magick, philosophy, religion, and spirituality can come together, supporting our transition into this next phase of evolution.

The Three Rays of Witchcraft is my contribution to a new body of lore, synthesizing past traditions into a new, modern view of the Craft. It is my vision, incorporating elements that have been the most meaningful and transformative while remaining true to my Craft roots. Though it is not a work for beginners, and is intended for those who have some experience but are looking to go deeper or simply in another direction, I've done my best to explain basic concepts as needed without getting mired in the basics, so I can focus on the new concepts. We all have different backgrounds and educations, but the ultimate purpose is to present a new system of magick and expand our current philosophy and put it into practical application. May it catalyze your own visions, your own missions, in this and all other worlds.

PART ONE:
KNOWLEDGE
OF
THE
VISION

CHAPTER ONE:
THE TRIUNE DIVINITY

And one day, towards the end of the year, as Ceridwen was culling plants and making incantations, it chanced that three drops of the charmed liquor flew out of the cauldron and fell upon the finger of Gwion Bach. —Taliesin

In my vision of the three rays of Witchcraft, the first element of the mandala image was three drops. These three darkened circles initially represent the three drops of awen found in the Druidic and Bardic traditions. In the tale of Taliesin the Bard, the boy Gwion Bach is a servant to the Witch Ceridwen, who is brewing a magickal potion. The potion is for her son Avagddu, whose name means "utter darkness." His sister Creirwy is the epitome of beauty, but he is the opposite. Avagddu is the ugliest boy in the world, and although Ceridwen's magick cannot break the curse of his looks, she can give him the gift of awen, of inspiration. This inspiration doesn't manifest simply as ideas, but also as poetry and eloquence, knowledge and wisdom, magick, prophecy, and power.

The concept of awen is connected to life force and power, the power of the gods that flows on the wind and descends from the heavens. It is the breath of life that feeds the bard or Druid's "Fire in the Head," a sign of deity-touched inspiration and magick. Some equate it with other words that link breath, air, and life force, such as *prana* from India or *pneuma* from the Greek, but awen is much more than life force. It is the knowledge and wisdom to put that power into action. Such action often takes form in words and poetry that change the people and the world around the poet.

So if Ceridwen's son cannot have physical beauty to naturally charm people, then her gift of wisdom and power will make him beloved despite his looks. She brews the potion in her cauldron in a hut on the island of Tegid Voel, where she resides with her giant husband, whom the island is named after. Although not always clear, it is assumed that she, too, is a giant, as they are both primal powers, elder gods akin to the Titans of Greek myth. Ceridwen instructs Gwion Bach to continually stir the potion while a blind man named Morda keeps the fire going. The potion is known as greal, and might link the cauldron to the later imagery of the grail popular in Arthurian myth. Ceridwen fares forth into the world for a year and a day to collect the necessary herbs and roots for the potion, harvesting them at specific places and times, in accord with the stars.

The potion reaches a critical point while Ceridwen is away. The boiling liquid rises, and three drops scald Gwion's thumb. Instinctively he sucks his thumb, a motion later to become a ritual trigger gesture for bards, and he immediately receives all the potion's magick. The three drops of awen, from the greal, contain all its power. The rest of the brew turns poisonous, cracks the cauldron, and flows out from the hut, poisoning the land and water. Those three drops initiate a tremendous magickal change in Gwion Bach. He immediately knows the serious-ness of his plight, for the Witch goddess Ceridwen will know what has happened, and hunt him down.

Gwion runs and uses his newfound magickal power to shapeshift through the elements as Ceridwen matches each transformation and keeps up with him. He becomes a hare, and she becomes a greyhound. He becomes a fish, and she matches him in the form of an otter. He becomes a bird, and she almost catches him as a hawk. He thinks he's clever and transforms into a grain of wheat in a pile of grain on the thrashing floor of a granary, hidden, almost invisible, but Ceridwen becomes a black hen and devours him. Nine months later, she gives birth to him, and while she desires to murder him for his seeming betrayal, she casts him upon the weir in a leather bag, to float along the water. He eventually finds a new family and home, is immediately named Taliesin, or "shining brow," by his rescuer, Elphin, and begins his own adventures.

What at first simply seems like a myth of a terrible goddess and a boy who escapes her wrath is revealed to be an initiatory story between teacher and student, or goddess and potential bard. Each part of the tale has initiatory meaning. Gwion Bach is making a potion for the dark child, who is balanced by a light child. Some would argue that all three are aspects of the same individual. Gwion is not only Ceridwen's servant and slave but in some ways another son. His siblings are aspects of himself. He spends a year and a day in a dark hut, performing repetitive acts with a blind man. Many Witches, modern and traditional, undergo periods of training for the classic Celtic year and a day, which in many ways is a time of meditation, ritual, and learning plant lore and potion brewing from a master. One can look at Gwion's shapeshifting journey as a trial through the elements of fire, water, air, and earth. Then the initiate is reborn after a further process, through the gates of the Goddess, her very womb. He is cast out to test his mettle and find his own way like a newborn babe, literally reborn. But what initiates this sequence of true mystery training is the three drops of awen.

In my own awen mandala vision, the three drops embody the three primal powers, the three seeds that initiate all magick. It is the triune divinity and all that it embodies expressed in three perfect drops of greal. In ritual, the word is chanted in three parts, Ah-oo-en, to emphasize the triune nature of its mystery.

While most Witches identify as polytheists, meaning they worship many gods and not just one, those who also identify with the rich Western occult tradition recognize an overarching spirit running throughout creation. In the Hermetic tradition this one spirit can be called the Divine Mind. Eastern-influenced practitioners might think of it as the Tao. Those with more tribal leanings might call it the Great Spirit. This one spirit has many expressions, including all the gods and goddesses of paganism, all of the known world and therefore all of us. Most of us think of the primary expression of the divine spirit as two. We see things in terms of polarity and complements: male and female, light and dark, and even up and down. The Tao is divided into yin and yang, though each contains the seed of the other. In Witchcraft the divine is seen as both Goddess and God. In fact, my own tradition calls the divine parents "the Two who move as One in the Love of the Great Spirit." But one of the most helpful expressions of this divine spirit occurs when it is divided by three. The two forces are mediated by a third.

The three primary mystical principles are those of creation, sustainment, and destruction (chart 1). This triple pattern is found time and again in mythology and philosophy to describe the primal power of divinity. In fact, one of my very first teachers described God as an acronym. The G stands for "generating." It is the power that initiates creation and begins all processes. Something is generated from this power where once there was nothing. The O stands for "organizing." This power shapes what is created, giving it form and pattern, allowing it to sustain itself over time. The final power, D, stands for "dissolution" or "destruction." It is the power that destroys in order to return the basic components to creation to begin again.

GOD	Generating	Organizing	Dissolution
Astrology	Cardinal	Fixed	Mutable
Alchemy	Sulfur	Salt	Mercury
Hinduism	Brahma	Vishnu	Shiva
OM/AUM	A	U	M
Yogic philosophy	Rajas	Tamas	Sattva
Egyptian	Hu	Sia	Heka
Christianity	Father	Son	Holy Ghost
Ceremonial magick	Isis	Osiris	Apophis
Witchcraft	Maiden	Mother	Crone
Awen	Ah	Oo	En

CHART 1: TRIPLE PATTERNS

In looking at the art and science of astrology, the zodiac signs can be divided into three powers, called cardinal, fixed, and mutable. These are, respectively, the organizing, sustaining, and dissolving forces of astrology. When the Sun enters a cardinal sign, it initiates a season. Aries initiates spring, Cancer initiates summer, Libra initiates fall, and Capricorn initiates winter. When the Sun enters a fixed sign, it is the middle of a season. Taurus is the middle of spring, Leo is the middle of summer, Scorpio is the middle of fall, and Aquarius is the middle of winter. When the Sun enters a mutable sign, the season will soon end. Gemini is at the end of spring, Virgo is at the end of summer, Sagittarius is at the end of fall, and Pisces is at the end of winter. Here, the four seasons each undergo a threefold process of birth, life, and death.

In alchemy, the three forces are looked upon as the chemicals sulfur, mercury, and salt. They are not literally these chemicals, but each chemical is representative of one of the triune powers. Sulfur is the energy of combustion, of light and projection. Considered solar in nature, it is the first spark, the first moment of creation and generation, as the chemical sulfur is flammable. Mercury is the energy of dissolution, of reflection and receptivity. Considered lunar in nature, it is that which dissolves and breaks down form. The metal quicksilver is reflective and flowing, though toxic. Salt is the energy of the mediating force between the two extremes. It is the power of fixedness, solidity, and manifestation. In its most basic and familiar form, salt is a compound, NaCl, or sodium chloride, a combination of elements, while sulfur and mercury are pure elements, from a modern chemist's perspective.

In forms of Hinduism, the great cosmic god Brahman is divided into a trinity. Brahman, not to be confused with the priestly caste of Brahmin in India, is the great unchanging and infinite divine reality in which all of creation manifests. Brahman is divided into the creator god Brahma, who initiates the creation of the universe and all worlds seen and unseen; Vishnu, the preserver of the universe; and Shiva, who will ultimately dissolve or destroy the universe so it will be created again.

The Egyptian traditions have their own trinity of sorts through Hu, Sia, and Heka, related to the god Thoth as the one who issues forth the Divine Utterance. Hu is the spoken word, while Sia is omniscience, or divine knowledge. Heka is magick itself. Though not a perfect match by far, they could be seen as akin to the three forces of initiation, sustainment, and change.

Yogic philosophy, also based on the traditions in India, recognizes three states known as the *gunas*: rajas, tamas, and sattva. Guna literally means "string," "thread," or "twine," but its philosophical meaning is to categorize three basic tendencies, also associated with our triplicities. Rajas is associated with initiation and the cardinal signs, while tamas is linked with preservation and the fixed signs and thereby sattva with the mutable signs and dissolutions. Astrologers, however, don't assign a state of balanced perfection to the mutable signs, while Hindu philosophy associates sattva with perfection. The gunas are used in Aryurvedic medicine to determine body types and prescribe diets and medicines.

Christianity, too, has a divine trinity. Though the Christian trinity is not equated with these three esoteric principles by any mainstream Christian church, esoteric Christian mystics can easily draw parallels between the Father, Son, and Holy Spirit and our principles of creation, sustainment, and destruction. In these teachings, God the Father is undoubtedly the creator and initiator of all. God the Son, in the form of Jesus Christ, is the redeemer; he "saves" his followers. Some would see him as the preserving principle for this reason, though his prophesied Second Coming is said to initiate the end of the world, so he could be seen as the destructive element as well. The Holy Spirit, also known as the Holy Ghost and Holy Sophia, is the disguised wisdom principle, the spark in all things, and is considered either the preserving force sustaining the world or the spirit to which we shall all return upon the end of the universe.

Modern ceremonial magick's trinity comes in the form of a formulaic chant found in the Hexagram rituals of the Golden Dawn tradition and their various offshoots. It is written as IAO and chanted as Eee-Aah-Ooh. While it originally was a Gnostic chant derived from the Hebrew Tetragrammaton, YHVH, most practitioners today interpret the letters as standing for the Egyptian gods Isis, Apophis, and Osiris. In this formula, Isis is the Great Mother, the generating principle of creation and nature. Apophis is equated with Typhon and Set, the destructive and monstrous element of the mythos. Osiris is the resurrected god, redeeming nature, and thereby is equated with the sustaining power of our triad.

The Witchcraft traditions look at the great creative force personally as the Goddess, and see her in triple form. The Great Mother is most popularly seen today as the Maiden of the Moon and Heavens, the Mother of the Earth and Nature, and the Crone of the Underworld and Dead. She is seen as the Goddess of Fate, weavers or Wyrd sisters of the past, present, and future, spinning the thread, measuring the thread, and cutting the thread of life. The Greeks have their Moirae, or "Apportioners," with Clotho ("Spinner"), Lachesis ("Alotter"), and Atropos ("Inexorable"). The Roman counterpart is Parcae, or "Sparring Ones," with Nona ("Ninth"), Decima ("Tenth") and Morta ("Death"). The Norns of the Norse—Urd ("fate"), associated with the past; Verdandi ("happening"), associated with the present; and Skuld ("debt"), associated with the future—don't weave as much as they water the World Tree and divine patterns in the drops of water, preserving the Tree. Like the Greco-Roman fates, even the gods are subject to the power of the Fates. The Anglo-Saxons have their fates as the Wyrd sisters, popularized in Shakespeare's *Macbeth*, though no surviving English names appear for each. Shakespeare linked these three Witches to the Greek Witchcraft goddess Hecate, also seen as triple herself.

A variety of triple goddesses, both historical and with modern roots, are popular in Witchcraft today, including the Irish Morrighan triplicity of Anu, Babd, and Macha (or Babd Catha, Macha, and Nemain); the triple Bridgets of Ireland, embodying healing, poetry, and smithcraft; and the Welsh Goddess as embodied by Arianrhod, Blodeuwedd, and Ceridwen. In fact, as we explore the races of the three rays later in this text, we'll find that three of the most popular images of the Goddess create a new triune view of the Great Mother. Through the first ray she will embody the Goddess of War and Battle. Through the second ray she is both the Goddess of Love and the Goddess of Nature. With the third ray she is the Goddess of Animals, of the Herd and Hunt.

All of these mythologies show us the triple power, the essence of creation, and I believe that understanding is the cornerstone of the magick transferred to Taliesin. What is magick but the power to create, to sustain your creation, and to break things down so something new can be built? These three "drops" are the seeds to be planted in the aspiring Witch, magician, or bard, for we must know the primal powers, and be in touch with their essence within, before attempting to effect change in the apparent outer world. These three drops are the necessary first step. They must be distilled from the essence of nature, yet once you know these primal powers, you will see them everywhere and in everything. Then you will be ready to align yourself with them in the worlds of matter and spirit.

Three drops from the Cauldron of Creation.
Three drops from the Cauldron of Inspiration.
Three drops of light ushering forth from the cosmic womb.
Creation, sustainment, dissolution.
Creation, destruction, evolution.
Creation from the source of all that is, was, and ever will be.
Three seeds planted within the soil of time.
Three seeds planted within the soul shrine.
Three seeds bearing fruit of the will, heart, and mind.
The magick of awen flowing free.

CHAPTER TWO:
THE TRIUNE CREATION

The three states of living beings: Annwn, whence the beginning;
Abred, in which is the increase of knowledge, and hence goodness;
and Gwynvyd, in which is the plenitude of all goodness, knowledge,
truth, love, and endless life. —The three states from *The Barddas*
of Iolo Morganwg

The three primary powers that are embodied in the three drops of awen must manifest a universe in which to create. Many esoteric systems and philosophies attempt to map the metaphysical cosmos, with the intention to help humanity understand our place within the cosmos, and give us a guide to where we have been and where we are going. In fact, that could be considered the primary purpose of all religions, both exoteric and esoteric: we want to know who we are, why we are here, and where to go or what to do next. Complex cosmological maps have been created by practitioners of many traditions, including ancient Greek philosophers and their post-Christian Neoplatonist spiritual inheritors, Jewish Kabbalists with the Tree of Life, and even Eastern Taoist masters with their heavenly and terrestrial hierarchies. Such maps help us navigate the territory but shouldn't be confused with the territory itself. When you confuse your map, be it a personal cosmology or traditional religious doctrine, for the truth of reality rather than an interpretation of it, you stumble into dogma and might never get out of its trap.

Whenever I look at a magickal concept, I look for its cognates across space and time. I look to what is essential in the human condition. There I find truth. If traditions have worked independently with certain concepts in different times and cultures, then there is something fundamental about that concept and its relationship to the human spiritual, magickal, or religious experience. To see this principle in action, we need only look at the similarities of rituals around the world, each with a different cultural connotation and theological meaning yet having much the same underlying ritual "technology." In function, the Catholic High Mass isn't so different from a Wiccan Moon Circle, even if the philosophies, cultures, and attitudes informing the ritual actions are different.

A cosmological thread of truth is the division of three. While there are many more complex ways of dividing reality into territories on a map, the basic model of three zones is repeated and expanded upon in many different cultures. The classic archetypal image found across the planet is a spiritual realm above us or beyond us, extending off the planet into the depths of space and the heights of the heavens; a spiritual realm below us, extending within the planet and unknown subterranean realms; and the world in which humanity currently resides, a world between the two other realms, the world of space, time, nature, and life. These realms are known as the Upper World, Middle World, and Lower World, or the Overworld, Middle World, and Underworld. In some teachings, reality is divided into five realms, making distinctions between the Over/Upper and Under/Lower Worlds, viewing two distinct levels above and two distinct levels below. But for all practical purposes, they describe the same realms. I tend to use the terms interchangeably. While the Upper and Lower Worlds exist in directions we can literally point to, most modern scientists would lump all that can be seen, examined, measured, and tested into the world between, and designate the other two realms as fiction, or at the very least the purview of theologians. Yet to Witches, shamans, and magicians of any stripe, these worlds are just as real.

That global thread of truth shows us that the three worlds are connected by a spire, what is known as the *axis mundi*, or main axis, upon which the cosmos rotates. Each mythos describes this primary figure differently. Sometimes the axis is a mountain. Sometimes it is a ladder. Most often, particularly in Indo-European myth, the axis is a tree, though this image also is found in Asia, India, and the Americas. Some cultures name specific trees as holding the honor of being the World Tree. In Norse and Saxon traditions, it is an ash, or possibly a yew, while in Slavic and Finnish myth, it is an oak. The Celts also have strong associations with the oak tree, as the word *duir*, or oak, closely resembles the word Druid, the name of the religious-magical caste in Celtic culture. In some faery faith traditions, it is known as the Bile Tree. In Hinduism, it is the sacred fig named the ashvastha, while in Buddhism, it is the Bodhi Tree. Italian folkloric traditions also name the fig or walnut as a sacred faery tree, and the original concept of the faeries relates them to *fata*, or fate, the triple principle described by three drops of awen in the previous chapter.

The World Tree, which more appropriately should be named the Universal Tree, is the main axis connecting the realms above, below, and between. Typically the Tree is described as having its branches in Heaven, its trunk in the world, and its roots in the Underworld. A few exceptions, such as the Hindu ashvastha tree or some depictions of the Qabalistic Tree of Life, reverse the Tree, giving it roots in the Upper World and branches in either the Middle or Lower World, and emphasizing that the source of the Tree is in the heavens.

Various complex tree models have developed out of this simple image, from the Nine Worlds of Norse mythology, with the World Tree depicted as an ash named Yggdrasil, known as Irminsul to the Saxons, to the complex model of the Tree of Life in both Jewish and Hermetic lore.

In any depiction, the purpose of the Tree is not only to unite the worlds but also to give the magickal practitioner a means for traversing the worlds. Many stories involve figures climbing the Tree or crawling into the roots. The name Yggdrasil usually is translated as "Odin's horse," and could refer to the Norse god Odin's ordeal of hanging himself from the World Tree for nine days and nine nights in a sacrificial ritual to gain the wisdom of the runes and traverse the nine worlds. Odin is traditionally a gallows god, and the Tree is the method by which the hanged man hangs, giving him his journey to the spirit world.

For both the Celts and the Greeks, the image of the land, sky, and sea was used as a focus for the three worlds (chart 2). The Titan goddess Hecate, in addition to being a goddess of Witchcraft and enchantment, was said to rule a portion of each of these three realms. Anyplace where all three met, like the seashore, was considered magickally potent and between the worlds.

Culture	Upper Worlds	Middle Worlds	Lower Worlds
Christian	Heaven	Earth	Hell
Hebrew	Malkuth, Hashamaim	Assiah	Sheol, Gehenna
Celtic	Ceugant, Gwynvyd, Avalon	Bith, Mide, Abred	Annwynn/Annwn, Mag Mell, Tir na n-Og
Norse	Asgard, Alfheim	Midgard, Vanaheim, Jotunheim, Muspelheim	Helheim, Svartalfheim, Niflheim
Slavic	Irij, Parv	Iav	Nav, Peklo

CHART 2: THE THREE WORLDS

Culture	Upper Worlds	Middle Worlds	Lower Worlds
Finnish	—	—	Tuonela
Greek	Olympus	Gaia	Hades, Tartarus, Elysium
Roman	Olympus	Terra	Hades, Pluto, Avernus
Egyptian	Heliopolis, Aaru	Ta	Duat, Amenti, Neter-khertet, (Aaru)
Sumerian	An	Dilmun, Edinu	Abzu, Kur, Ki-Gal
Andean	Hanaq Pacha	Kay Pacha	Ukhu Pacha

CHART 2: THE THREE WORLDS (CONTINUED)

The model of the three worlds is found in indigenous traditions across the world steeped in what we would call shamanism. Shamanic cosmology can be found in preserved mythologies, as so many myth cycles relate the stories of the gods and heroes to the landscape of a heavenly world, a mortal realm, and an underworld.

The best-known image of the three worlds in our modern culture comes from Christian mythology, strangely paralleling its rival pagan religions. Essential mainstream Christian lore states that Heaven exists eternally above us and is reserved for the elect upon judgment. Only those who have "earned" the right to reside with God will be allowed entrance. Below us is Hell, where the damned will be punished in an underworld of torment, usually depicted as fire. Between these states is the Earth, where actions determine our final destination in Heaven or Hell. Although Christian esoterists would argue that this is a simplistic model of much more complex religious beliefs, it is the model most mainstream Christians and the general public know. What most modern practicing Christians don't know is that this model borrows much of its cosmology from the Persian religions, which were the first to emphasize such a drastic and moralistic division, and it also borrows terminology and imagery, such as Hell, originally Hel, from the Norse nine worlds.

We see similar zones, with different moralistic attitudes, in other pagan mythologies. The nine worlds of the Norse basically can be divided into three zones. The heavenly world is composed of Asgard, the home of the sky gods known as the Aesir, and possibly Alfheim, the home of the light elves. Valhalla, the hall of heroes, is found in Asgard. The middle zone consists of Midgard, or Middle Earth, and various zones around it, including Vanaheim, the realm of the Vanir nature gods, and Jotunheim, the land of giants. The Underworld has Svartalfheimr, the realm of the dark elves or dwarves, and Hel, or Helheim, the realm of the dead. The world of Muspelheim, the realm of fire, sometimes is described in the heavens and other times is described in the south around the Middle World, and likewise Niflheim, the realm of ice, is described either in the Underworld or in the north around the Middle World.

The ancient Greeks had three distinctive zones of reality, but not a specific axis mundi connecting all three of them. Folkloric Greek tradition depicts a tree with goblins gnawing at its roots, but the ancient myths have only Mount Olympus, connecting the gods to the world, and various caverns and entrances connecting the world to the realm of the dead.

Egyptian mythology, too, has three distinct realms, with the starry realm above, the black land of Egypt, and the realm of the dead. But beyond the temples, pyramids, and the Nile River, there is little to connect the three. Spiritual experience in the ancient pagan world is informed by the relationship with the landscape. In the deserts of Egypt, even amid the fertile Nile, there are no immense trees or mountains to connect the vertical axis, though the Egyptian pillar known as the djed, sacred to Osiris and associated with his spine, might have served as a mystical cosmic axis.

The triune model of creation doesn't always fall on the vertical axis, though for most us the concept of a vertical axis mundi is the more easily understandable. We relate to divinity and the spirit worlds in relationship to where we are, and the concept of a world out and above, a world within, and a world below makes sense due to our relative position on planet Earth. Cultures with open spaces would look at the largest spire, natural or even humanmade, as the conduit between these realms. Vertical spires have become ingrained in most of our thinking, as we are inheritors of the previous age's Piscean hierarchy, making models and systems with the concepts of above and below. We find this imagery in temples and churches with spires reaching for the heavens and in spiritual lineages descending from a supreme figure, such as the Catholic Pope, sitting at the top of an ecclesiastical hierarchy. We've modeled our businesses, governments, and society on similar principles, all spiritually grounded in the dual nature of Pisces. Its symbol is the two fish, both tied together, but one is swimming toward the heavens, or surface, and one is swimming toward the depths.

Our new models of structure soon will be drawn from Aquarian wisdom, whose hallmark is lateral relationships, the types found in circles, councils, and committees. Networks of individuals working to support each other have quickly become new and powerful moving forces in modern communication, particularly via the Internet. Cultures and societies that have looked at reality not as a vertical axis but as a horizontal concept will have much to teach. People in jungles and deep woods may not have a sense of the heavens and depths. Thick canopies cover the stars and make everything dark, so the model then becomes one not of above and below but of "here" and "there." The further out you get, the further you delve into another world.

One model of these worlds that speaks deeply to this type of cosmology is found in a controversial set of Welsh teachings based on the writings of Iolo Morganwg. In this model we have a Celtic cosmology of concentric rings. Born Edward Williams, this Welsh nationalist was a major figure in the nineteenth-century Druidic revival and was considered controversial for a number of reasons. He held revolutionary views in terms of his Welsh national pride, proposed that the Welsh explorer Madoc was the true discover of the United States, and was a talented forger of ancient Welsh texts.

Morganwg collected and transcribed a number of medieval Welsh texts and had a passion for Welsh myth, poetry, and culture. His work was collected from manuscripts by editor John Williams Ab Ithel and released as *The Barddas of Iolo Morganwg*. While this work is supposedly based on traditional texts and oral traditions from his extensive collection of authentic bardic lore, most scholars believe much of it, if not all, was his own invention, influenced by his own particular Christian views mixed with Welsh and pseudo-Welsh teachings. Morganwg's ability to forge documents, as well as the fact that much of the *Barddas* was written while he was under the influence of laudanum (opium), which he was taking as a medication for his asthma, makes it suspect, yet strangely this document is filled with poetic and visionary truths, if not literal translations of traditional lore. The work resonates with a variety of visionary texts, both traditionally accepted ones, such as the lore of the Qabalah and the Vedic Upanishads, and the more controversial *Prophecies of Merlin*. The *Barddas* contain a complex and comprehensive theology, cosmology, and, with its alphabet based on the runes and ogham symbols, magickal system.

Morganwg influenced both William Blake and Robert Graves, as well as the modern Druidic revival and various branches of neopaganism, Witchcraft, and British magick. If his cosmology and terminology were not a part of traditional folklore, they appear to have been adopted as genuine material by at least some Native Welsh traditional healers, Witches, and magicians. If Morganwg's material was not based on an ancient folkloric tradition, then his modern inspiration certainly has been woven into today's traditions.

In Morganwg's cosmology, adopted by many neopagan and new Celtic shamanic traditions, reality is described as concentric rings, and the evolution of an entity is the journey of passing through these rings to reach the outermost one (figure 1).

In the center of this model, at the beginning, is Annwn. Annwn is considered to be the Welsh Underworld, and means "the deep." Certainly Annwn is a part

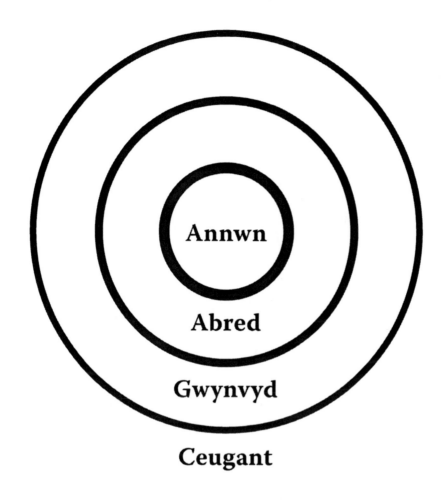

FIGURE 1: THE THREE RINGS OF CREATION

of traditional Welsh folklore, as Annwn (also spelled Annwyvn) is the name of the realm of the ruler Arawn, who trades places with Pwyll in the branch of *The Mabinogion* known as "Pwyll, Prince of Dyfed." Unlike the models with a vertical axis mundi, the threshold between worlds in this cosmology is a hedge, river, or clearing. Pwyll crossed into Annwn from his world by stumbling into a woodland glade he found while hunting a stag, not realizing he had entered another realm. He knew he was in another world only because of the otherworldly dogs that attacked the stag before his dogs could. They shone with brilliant whiteness and glistening red ears. There was no climb or obvious transition point, but rather a gentle passing from one world to the next, as if through some unseen and insubstantial veil. Some describe Annwn as the realm of the first and primal cauldron of the Goddess, from which all things flow. We get our start here, crawling out of the cauldron. If we are not successful on our journey to the outer ring, we may find ourselves returned to the cauldron, cooked and broken down so someone or something new can form and make the journey again.

The second realm in this model of concentric rings is known as Abred, the realm of mortals and what we tend to think of as the Middle World. Here, we learn, and by learning we become better and can potentially pass through to the next ring. This is the world in which all things are familiar to us: time, space, nature, and the seasons. Here is the realm of mortal concerns and the growth and trials we undergo.

The third realm in this model is Gwynvyd, the realm of immortals. According to Morganwg, it is the realm of "all goodness, knowledge, truth, love, and endless life." This is the world of those who have become like the gods, like the enlightened sages and scholars, whom we call the Mighty Dead or Hidden Company in the Witchcraft traditions. This is the realm of the saints, the bodhisattvas, the demigods, and Justified Ones. Here are the ceremonial magicians' Withdrawn Order, Inner Plane Adepts, and Secret Chiefs, or the Theosophists' Lords and Ladies of Shamballa, the Ascended Masters of the Great White Brotherhood. Gwynvyd is home to the masters of what I call the Timeless Tradition of the Nameless Art.

Though Annwn, Abred, and Gwynvyd complete our three-ring cosmology, there is said to be a state of Ceugant, or absolute divinity, surrounding the three realms, where one becomes one with "God" as the Creator if this state is reached.

The Three Rings of Creation

In my vision of the three rays of Witchcraft, the entire mandala was encircled by not one, but three, rings, as if the drops and rays were emanating from the center, from the cosmic cauldron of Annwn, but poised to work their magick in all three realms, reaching Ceugant. This mimics the traditional image of the rays of awen, also typically encircled by three rings.

Such a figure is reminiscent of an Irish figure known as Fionn's Window (figure 2), from the text *The Book of Ballymote*. Fionn's Window depicts five concentric circles marked with ogham alphabet lines. Modern practitioners, such as Edred Thorsson in his text *The Book of Ogham*, suggest this window is a two-dimensional depiction of the spirit worlds, where the three rings are depicted by the center, third, and fifth circles, and the two intermediary rings, the second and fourth, represent the connections between the Upper and Middle Worlds and the Middle and Lower Worlds. Each of the three worlds is divided into five provinces, or spiritual territories, marked by the four directions and the center. Each of the connecting rings also is divided into five, depicting five paths between the upper and middle realms and five paths between the middle and lower realms. Each of the ogham symbols represents a spiritual province or a connection zone between provinces, creating a form of Celtic "Qabalah" with Fionn's Window. This text gives us a Celtic vision of the spirit worlds in the form of concentric rings. The figure is reminiscent of Plato's vision of Atlantis, an ancient and inspiring city of five rings surrounded by canals and waterways. Such an image and a myth play a role in the Witchcraft teachings of the mysterious Coven of Atho written about by Doreen Valiente.

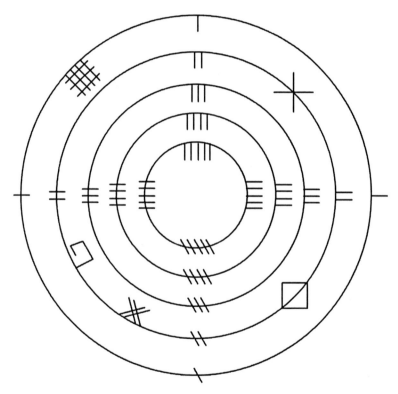

FIGURE 2: FIONN'S WINDOW

Fionn's Window usually is extended into a vertical "tree" image whereby the concentric rings on a horizontal plane are transformed into a vertical axis. This reminds us that neither a vertical nor a horizontal image of reality is quite true. Both are viewpoints that express different elements of truth regarding the three spiritual worlds. We have to find the spiritual maps that are most helpful to us today, drawing from the past but forging our own future. I believe we need models of reality that encompass both vertical and horizontal organizations of the Otherworld, and by holding the paradox of both, we find ourselves closer to truth.

Crawl out of the cauldron,
Creatures unfleshed.
Come out from the roots,
Pass the thorny hedge,
And enter the world of breath and blood,
The world of flesh and bone.
Be born again between Heaven and Hell.
Crawl out of the wood and clay,
And burn with illumination.
Fuel the fire,
And cross the veil of stars and gods.
Become one with the spirits of the heavens,
In the branches of the trees.
And reach beyond the realm of the known,
Storming the gates of mystery,
And touch the infinite.

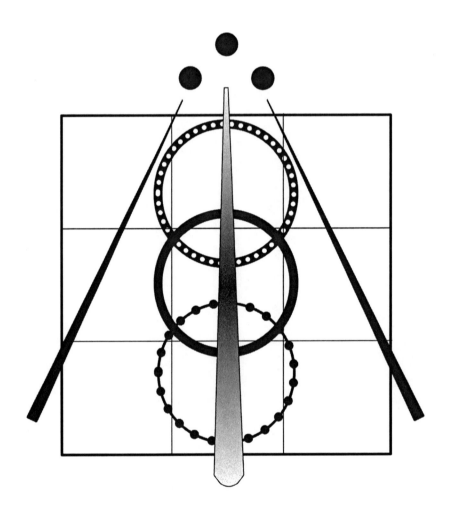

CHAPTER THREE:
THE TRIUNE POWERS

By a bent line, by a straight line, by a crooked line. —An old Craft saying

Three drops contain the three primary aspects of creation. Three rings encircle the three divine energies, creating the landscapes, the spiritual territories, where the three powers manifest. The only thing left to decipher from my vision of the three rays of Witchcraft is the manifestation of the divine energy. The three potential principles must be brought into action. They must emanate forth and do their work in the worlds. Their emanations form three paths, three roads, which simultaneously lead back to the source, to the divine creative spirit, and outward to the vast fields of potential, of creation, where we live, explore, and grow.

The most basic application of the three divine energies in manifestation is found in the Hindu teaching of Om. Many of us are familiar with the symbol and sound of OM, said to be the primary mantra of creation, the archetypal voice of the Brahman, ushering forth into creation.

Christian mystics will find parallels with the Logos, the Word of God, emanating outward to create the cosmos in the Judeo-Christian creation story, and the Word of God is later made manifest in the figure of Jesus Christ. God said, "Let there be light," and there was light. Whatever God spoke came into manifestation.

In the beginning was the Word, and the Word was with God,
and the Word was God. —John 1:1

The Hindu teaching on the "Word" has a hidden aspect to it. Chanted by many as a focus for meditation, healing, and harmony, Om practiced as a mantra quickly reveals its triune nature. Om is more appropriately written as Aum, or A, U, M, for a sustained intoning of the mantra clearly shows these three parts. *A* is the aspect of Braham. As it initiates the mantra, it stands for the initiation of creation. Coincidently, *A* is the start of our alphabet, the alpha of the Greeks. The *U* is the vowel sound that sustains the mantra. It is held the longest as the *A* sound slides gently into the *U*, prolonging the chant. Thus, the *U* is the tone of Vishnu, the preserver. Lastly, the *M* is the consonant that closes the mouth and ends the mantra, relating it to the principle of Shiva. The chant of Aum puts these three

Severity   Mildness   Mercy

FIGURE 3: THE TREE OF LIFE AND THE THREE PILLARS

creative forces into action. Reciting it aligns the practitioner with these powers, much like the Qabalistic formula of IAO.

Qabalists also have a clear teaching on three rays emanating from the divine source. Technically there are ten clear emanations, also known as *sephiroth*, from three "negative veils of existence" representing the divine in its most remote and unknowable form. Yet the ten sephiroth are neatly organized in various zones and categories. One of the easiest teachings to clearly see on the Tree of Life glyph is the Three Pillars (figure 3). On top of the Tree image are three sephiroth relating roughly to Goddess, God, and Great Spirit. Each one heads one of the Three Pillars.

On the left side of the Tree is the Pillar of Severity. Topped by Binah, the black sephira of understanding that corresponds with Saturn, the planet of karma and limitations, the Pillar of Severity mediates the difficult and destructive forces of the universe. Binah is followed by Geburah, the red sephira of might or power corresponding to Mars, and Hod, the orange sephira of splendor and communication corresponding to Mercury.

On the right side of the Tree is the Pillar of Mercy. Topped by Chokmah, the gray sephira of wisdom that corresponds to the zodiac and possibly the planet Neptune, the Pillar of Mercy mediates the benevolent and kind forces of the universe. Chokmah is followed by Chesed, also known as Gedulah, the blue sephira of mercy and kindness corresponding to Jupiter, and Netzach, the green sephira of victory, of love, passion, and sensuality, corresponding to Venus.

The central pillar is the Pillar of Mildness, which is topped by Kether, the dazzling white sephira with the name that means "the crown" and corresponds to the Divine Spirit, both male and female. Some equate this sephira with Pluto, while others correspond it to Uranus. It is the balancing force between Severity and Mercy. Each one unchecked would ruin the universe. Destruction without compassion is cruel and ultimately pointless when there is no need for it. Compassion without limits is just as bad, for no boundaries are drawn, nothing gets done, and everything melts together in an undifferentiated mess.

Each point on the Pillar of Mildness mediates between the sephiroth of the two outer pillars. Kether is followed by Tiphereth, the golden yellow sephira that is ruled by the Sun. It is the power of harmony, light, and self-sacrifice. Below Tiphereth is the sphere of the Moon, Yesod, which forms the spiritual or astral foundation for all physical manifestation. Lastly, at the bottom of the Tree, the "fruit," if you will, is Malkuth, the kingdom, balanced by four directions and elements, with four colors—black, olivine, russet, and citrine. It is the realm of manifestation, what we think of as the Earth or the material universe.

The Three Pillars of the Tree of Life fit nicely into other Hermetic myths stating that Hermes has two pillars that contain all knowledge. Here the secret teachings were preserved throughout the ages, from Atlantis, to Egypt, to the sacred temples of the Hebrew Holy of Holies. The two pillars are Boaz and Jachin, the two copper pillars of Solomon's First Temple and now preserved in the tarot and Masonic Rite. They represent the extremes of polarity, light and dark, Sun and Moon, fire and water, Capricorn and Cancer. Yet humans are called to be the third pillar, the middle pillar mediating between the two forces. Only then will the mysteries be revealed. Together, the three pillars fit nicely into our will (Severity), love (Mercy), and wisdom (Mildness) trinity. Study of each pillar can give us greater understanding of the alternating current for these forces as they emanate from the divine source into the human world.

Practitioners in the modern New Age movement, specifically those involved with ascension practices, have a triune power structure as established in the science of the seven rays. Though many think of the science of the seven rays as a dressed-up form of color magick or some model based on recent teachings regarding the seven chakras, in truth it is a much more theologically complex system based on the Theosophically inspired writings of Alice Bailey. The Spiritualist Church movement, the Theosophical Society of Madame Blavatsky, and the writings of Alice Bailey published by Lucius Trust laid the foundation for much of the New Age movement, though many casual practitioners are not aware of these roots. As this material rose to popular consciousness through publication in the days of the ceremonial magick movement, it was incorporated into the terminology of ceremonial magicians such as Dion Fortune, though with different terminology and definitions than Bailey.

In the book *The Rays and the Initiations*, Bailey outlines a complex structure of "rays," each embodying an archetypal force. Rather than using the model of the rainbow, which many assume is the case when they hear "seven rays," Bailey's model is based on the primary and secondary colors. Three primary archetypal forces, or Rays of Aspect, are outlined, and from the third ray emanates the remaining four Rays of Civilization, embodying the more human experience. Each ray is associated with one of the ascended masters of this tradition, and provides the framework for a more complex spiritual hierarchy, including many more entities holding "offices," or positions, within the hierarchy, which change as they, too, evolve and grow. According to Bailey's channeled writings, this was the secret spiritual science taught in the deepest recesses of Tibet. Interestingly enough, although probably not intentional, the three primary ray colors match the colors associated with the "three jewels" of Buddhism—red, blue, and gold.

The first of the rays is the red ray, the ray of will. It is associated with warriors and kings and ultimately embodies the true purpose. In a more modern context, it is the ray of the politician, executive, and explorer, as well as the occultist, who is essentially a mystical explorer. The red ray is the power of action and, when necessary, force and can bring the qualities of courage and statesmanship. The planetary "office" or entity who rules over the highest attributes of the red ray is known as the Manu, a name taken from Hinduism for the archetypal human, similar to the Qabalistic concept of the Adam Kadmon. The entity in the office of the Manu is responsible for the evolution of humanity and, in particular, for guiding the formation or the dissolution of racial, social, cultural, and governmental groups, and also oversees the development of the continents on the Earth's crust.

The second of the rays is the blue ray, the ray of love. This can seem like a strange association for many magicians, as we tend to use green or pink as the color of love, but in this Theosophical model it is a higher vibration of love, what Witches call Perfect Love. The blue ray also has been called a ray of spiritual education, for love is the cornerstone of this education. This ray is associated with teachers, healers, sages, and those who selflessly serve humanity. It embodies the power of love, healing, peace, intuition, and spiritual initiation. The entity who rules over the highest attributes of the blue ray is known as the Planetary Christ, a highly charged term for those of us who do not follow a Christian tradition. This name simply indicates an entity who embodies and mediates the Christos principle, or Christ consciousness, in the world. It could easily be named for any other selfless spiritual icon. For those with a ceremonial magick background, it could be called solar consciousness or Tiphereth consciousness. The Planetary Christ is considered to be the World Teacher, the spirit who grounds the teachings of the age into form.

The third of the rays is known as the yellow ray, the ray of active intelligence. Active intelligence is the ability to put knowledge into action, and has been called by many the power of wisdom, but some texts describe the blue ray as the ray of wisdom, creating confusion. The third ray also is known as the ray of civilization or the ray of humanity, for the subsequent four rays find their root in it. It is the ray of anyone who uses their knowledge, and archetypes range from the philosopher to the astrologer, mathematician, economist, and historian. The yellow ray embodies abstract ideas, communication, creativity, planning, and ultimately the power to manifest ideas into reality, ideally considered a human trait. It can be considered the essence of simple magick, popularized in its most basic form as the law of attraction or positive thinking. The entity who rules the highest aspects of this ray is the Mahachohan, or "much master," and is titled the Lord of Civilization. Each of the seven rays has a chohan, or master, who guides its use and development, acting as teacher and healer to both spirits and human initiates. The Mahachohan is the guide to these seven chohan, and also works with all manner of spirits in nature to guide the development of the planet's civilization.

We could sum up the three primary rays as the powers of thinking (yellow), feeling (blue), and doing (red). The remaining four rays are the green ray of harmony through conflict, the orange ray of technology and science, the indigo ray of devotion and religion, and the violet ray of ceremonial order. Each plays a role in the spiritual hierarchy, representing a different path to initiation and development, but they remain secondary to the red, blue, and yellow rays.

While researching traditional and modern teachings on Druidism, I came across the symbol of awen used by the Order of Bards, Ovates and Druids, or OBOD (figure 4). Though this symbol didn't strike me strongly upon first exposure, it obviously worked deep within my psyche, as it influenced my own vision of the three rays of Witchcraft. The image of three points of light with three rays descending was originally created, as far as we know, by Iolo Morganwg, but it has been adopted into many Druidic traditions, often with the three circles for the three worlds of creation. The three dots are said to be the three points at which the sun rises and sets on the equinoxes and solstices, called the Triad of the Sunrises. If you looked at the sun rise at one of these points from behind a standing stone, it would give you one of the "rays" by its shadow (figure 5). By putting together the shadows of summer solstice, equinox, and winter solstice, we have the three rays of awen. The three lines relate to the realms of earth, sea, and sky; the trinity

FIGURE 4: DRUIDIC AWEN SYMBOL

of truth, love, and wisdom; the trinity of knowledge, thought, and inspiration; as well as the vowels of awen: I, O, and U.

According to the *Barddas*, the three rays of awen also are said to be the three shouts of the creator god, known as Celi in this Druidic teaching. Awen, like Aum, is divided into three syllables: Ah-Oo-En. Einigan the Giant, whom some would paint as a Welsh cognate to Enoch in terms of spiritual initiation, saw the three rays of awen. He saw and heard them at the same time, and recorded them as three lines. The lines formed the letters O-I-W, which stood for the creator god, for the true name of Celi, but they could not be pronounced without "misnaming" God, much like the Qabalistic teachings of YHVH. The rays formed the basis of awen.

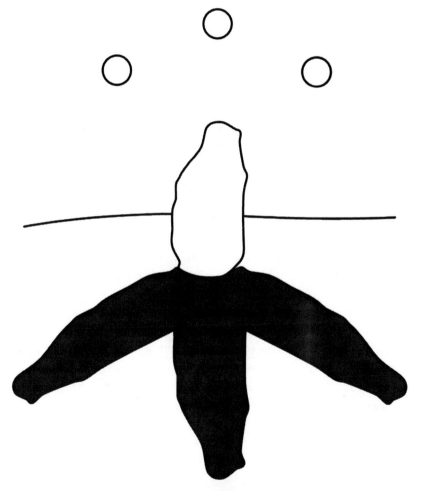

FIGURE 5:
AWEN CREATED THROUGH THE SHADOW OF A STANDING STONE

Einigan was the first to understand the three rays of Celi. He knew there were three levels of learning to awen. It must be seen, heard, and written to be fully understood. In understanding all knowledge, Einigan wrote it down using an alphabet of straight and slanted lines, what we would know as the ogham, upon three staves of rowan. He drove the staves into the ground, imitating and mirroring the three rays. Instead of descending from the heavens, they rose from the earth. Those who came after him misunderstood. Instead of learning the knowledge written on the staves, they worshiped the staves as gods themselves. Einigan was so disheartened by the actions of his fellow men that his heart burst and he died on the spot. A year and day later, Menw, the son of Menwyd or Teirgwaedd, who in Theosophical terms could be seeing as the archetypal human, Manu, came upon the three staves, growing right out of the skull of the giant. He took the staves, learned their knowledge, and passed it on to others of the Druidic tradition. The wisdom of the three rays was passed from the divine to the first race of giants, of Titans, and through the death of the giants, the knowledge was regenerated and passed on to humanity.

The three rays also relate to three mythical figures considered to be the first bards or Druids of Britain, named Gwron, Plennydd, and Alawn. Each figure and ray embodies a particular aspect of awen. Gwron is the knowledge of awen and is the ray on the left of the symbol. It represents the Sun's lowest point at the winter solstice and corresponds to the rank of the bard. Bards gather knowledge and lore. Plennydd is the power of awen. It is the ray to the right of the image and represents the Sun's highest point at the summer solstice. Plennydd corresponds to the rank of the Ovate, who experiences nature directly. Alawn is the peace of awen. It is the middle ray of the Sun's midpoint and both equinoxes. It is representative of the rank of the Druid, who brings peace and balance through uniting knowledge and power.

While the Druidic symbol of awen gave some intellectual understanding of these three emanations, the first time I came into contact with this concept in a tradition more akin to Witchcraft was in the Scottish tale *Thomas the Rhymer*, or True Thomas, introduced to me through the work of author R. J. Stewart. In *Thomas the Rhymer*, the Faery Queen takes Thomas beyond the Living Land, and while resting together she shows him the three roads.

O see ye not that narrow road,
So thick beset with thorns and briers?
That is the path of righteousness,
Tho after it but few enquires.

And see not ye that braid braid road,
That lies across that lily leven?
That is the path to wickedness,
Tho some call it the road to heaven.

And see not ye that bonny road,
That winds about the fernie brae?
That is the road to fair Elfland,
Where thou and I this night maun gae.

The Faery Queen outlines three paths, three potential ways beyond the realm of the living that we might describe as magickal or religious initiatory paths. Each embodies a different energy, from the perspective of a Scottish Faery faith tradition surviving at least in folkloric consciousness.

There is the road of briars and thorns, narrow and tight. Only small animals pass easily through the hedge of briars, so it is named the path of righteousness, as it's a path of suffering, though some find illumination through suffering. The Faery Queen plainly states that there are only "few enquires."

The second road is wide and smooth and looks quite easy. Some think of it as the road to Heaven, the road everybody takes, the easy path, but the Faery Queen lets Thomas know it is truly a path to wickedness.

The third and final road is a path of flowers and delights, which leads to Elfland, the Faery Queen's own realm. This is the territory of an elder race of beings in greater harmony with the land, who withdrew from the surface world yet maintain links with it through people such as True Thomas.

With further meditation, I learned that the three trees held sacred in so much British folklore—oak, ash, and thorn—also could describe the three powers. Oak is strong and straight and is associated with the first ray. It is a tree of the strong warrior gods and sky kings. The ash is considered an otherworldly tree in many traditions. Ash has some associations with the faery realm, though we might think the third tree, either hawthorn or blackthorn, has more faery associations. Yet in myth, it is the smaller briar tree, the thorn, that stands between the oak and the ash, as both a barrier and a connecting gateway, like the serpent in the vision of the three rays. The thorn, both white and black, also has associations with Witchcraft, magick, and medicine, making it appropriate for our crooked path. Even its physical manifestation, white and black, healing and poisonous, reveals the dual nature of the third ray.

The last bit of information I received to help me understand the vision of awen came not from modern Wicca but from those Witches who identify as Traditional Witches, coming from what they believe to be a pre-Gardnerian line.

As in the poetry of True Thomas, these Witches described three roads or three lines. The first was a straight line, narrow and true. This related to the mysteries of the sacred king and the dragon of the land. The second was a bent line calling those who are faery touched. The last was the Witch's path, the crooked line of cunning and unmaking. Another variation of this is found in the saying "By a bent line, by a straight line, by a crooked line." According to Peter Paddon, Traditional Craft publisher (Pendraig Publishing) and host of *the Crooked Path* podcast, the bent line is the circle, or the warded sacred space of the working. The straight line is the Bile Tree, another name for the axis mundi so often represented by the stang, or forked staff, in Traditional Craft. The crooked line is the serpent power, the dragon path of the earth energies through the three realms. These three lines explained from the context of Witchcraft touched something deep inside me, but it was only later that I got a fuller view of what they unlocked. Eventually they became a core part of my own personal cosmology and, along with the symbol of awen, the lynchpin for further synthesis among my Witchcraft, ceremonial magick, and Theosophical practices.

In my vision of the three rays, I saw the three sacred drops with three stylized lines projecting forth from them. I saw the three drops and the three rays surrounded by three circles, knowing the power of the three rays emanate forth from the cauldron in the heart of the Underworld and extend through the three realms, operating in each of the spiritual lands, making the scope of awen ninefold. I knew instantly that this vision was both a system of magick for material purposes and a holy sorcery for initiation into the mysteries and understanding our purpose in the world. It joined together my disparate traditions into something whole and new, yet with foundations in the past to support it.

The ray on the left was a straight line with a point, stylized into a weapon of some kind, perhaps a spear or an arrow. Instantly I knew it was the power of the straight line, which was the Pillar of Severity and the red ray of will. It its primary form it is the red ray, yet in the realm above it is still the color red. In the middle realm its color is gold, and in the lower realm its color is white. This ray is the expression of divine will and power, in harmony with the angelic and archangelic races who are an embodiment of divine will. It is sharp and pointed, single-focused. It is unyielding and unbending in purpose. In the manifest world it is mineral and metallic life, most like angels, for they, too, are the most unyielding in their form and purpose, the most patient in their evolution and development, the most like how they were when they were created.

The ray on the right was a curved line, like a branch of a tree, and trailing off of it were three flowers, one with four petals, one with five petals, and one with six. In its form I knew it was also the Pillar of Mercy and the blue ray of love. While blue might be its primary expression, in the upper realm it is the color blue, in the middle realm it is the color green, and in the lower realm it is the color black. It is an expression of divine love, the love we find in nature, unconditional, not sentimental. It is Perfect Love and Perfect Trust. The second ray is in harmony with the faery races, the spirits of nature that embody that divine natural attunement, be it above, below, or between. All of nature's intelligence, from the Underworld Sidhe to the spirits of flowers and trees and the devic entities that guide them, are part of the second ray. The four-petalled flower is for the Middle World and the four directions and four elements. The five-petalled flower is for the Lower World and the cycles of life and death. The six-petalled flower is for the Upper World and the six magickal planets—Moon, Mercury, Mars, Saturn, Jupiter, and Venus—with the Sun in the center.

The ray in the center was depicted as a serpent, crooked in shape, its coils undulating back and forth between the two other rays. The serpent was horned, much like the serpent held by the Celtic horned figure (often thought of as the god Cernunnos) on the Gunderstrup Cauldron (figure 6). On the brow of the serpent was the Witch star, a pentagram, and its tongue was forked. I knew this serpent was the embodiment of the third ray, the ray of active intelligence reforged as wisdom. While it is a golden yellow in its primary form, it, too, has three expressions. In the Upper World it is yellow gold, in the Middle World it is red, and in the Lower World it is scarlet. The serpent is the Pillar of Mildness, the balancing point between will/power and love/trust. Like the previous rays, it is dual in nature. It is not just wisdom, but also cunning—cunning in all senses, from the roots *cunnan* and *ken*, both meaning "to know," as well as the Cunning Man and Cunning Woman, the Witch or wisdom healer of a village. It is also cunning in the modern sense: shrewdness, ingenuity, skill, and craftiness. Our wisdom and cunning go hand in hand. The tongue is forked like the magickal blade is double-edged. Our words, our magick, have two sides of which we must always be aware.

The race of creatures associated with this third ray is not simply serpents, but also any of those creatures of flesh and blood that acquire wisdom and cunning. Such beings often are considered serpents, both in a positive sense, as in the case of the pythia, or prophetess, of the ancient Greek temple, and in a negative sense, when the snake's power is misunderstood and seen as deceptive. Such a negative portrayal of the serpent is depicted in the mainstream interpretation of the biblical Garden of Eden. The third ray is embodied by the creatures of flesh and blood, of all animal life. Humans embody the best and the worst this realm of flesh and blood has to offer.

As beings of the third, middle ray, the living creatures of flesh and blood exist between the realms of minerals and plants. Humanity stands between the angelic beings and the faery races. We have a unique role to play in the development of all three rays. While creatures of the first ray of Witchcraft, angels and mineral spirits, have no option other than divine will, for they are embodiments of it, we have to find and choose our divine will, what magicians refer to as the True Will or Mystic Will.

The nature spirits, devas, and fey of the second ray of Witchcraft have no option other than divine love, that intimate connection to nature and creation. We have to choose to love, and to refine that personal and sentimental love into divine love. We most often find divine love through a literal love and reverence of nature, where we understand that neither the clear and sunny day nor the thunderstorm is personal. Neither feast nor famine is personal. None is a reward or punishment. They are parts of the cycles of nature and the result of what has come before.

Humans exist within the third ray of Witchcraft. We undulate between action and desire, between will and love, until we find divine will and divine love. We must choose both. The choice is not automatic. In that journey, we gather knowledge, and as we apply that intelligence to choose both dvine will and divine love simultaneously, we find divine wisdom. It is through the union of these three powers, through humanity's ability to mediate the wide range of energies, that all races are connected and redeemed. We first find wisdom united with love and will for ourselves and our own personal development, and through our evolution we learn to be a bridge for the evolution of other entities. We form an alliance and then a gestalt, creating a triune being, and enter the next realm of consciousness together. The correspondences of the rays (chart 3) can give you a clear understanding of all the powers and entities associated with each energy.

The Theosophical model of reality doesn't end with the three primary Rays of Aspect, but also includes the four Rays of Civilization. Our own model of Witchcraft awen focuses only on three rays, but easily could be expanded to include all seven and beyond. The secondary rays are a mix of the three primary ray colors, and our understanding of them, too, is a mix of our three rays.

FIGURE 6: GUNDERSTRUP CAULDRON

PART ONE: KNOWLEDGE OF THE VISION

	First Ray	Second Ray	Third Ray
Theosophical ray:	First ray of will	Second ray of love	Third ray of intelligence
Traditional Craft:	Straight line	Bent line	Crooked line
Symbol:	Arrow/spear	Branch/plant	Serpent/lightning
Path:	Kings and warriors	Faery touched	Witches
Awen:	Thought	Knowledge	Inspiration
Tree:	Oak	Ash	Thorn
Pillar:	Severity	Mercy	Mildness
Meaning:	Will and Power	Love and Trust	Wisdom and Cunning
Divinity:	Divine will	Divine heart	Divine Mind
Beings of the Upper World:	Angelic races	Devas	Hidden Company
Beings of the Middle World:	Stone races	Nature spirits	Humans and animals
Kingdom:	Mineral	Vegetable	Animal
Beings of the Lower World:	Goetia	Faeries	Ancestors
Elevated color:	Red	Blue	Yellow gold
Base color:	Gold	Green	Scarlett
Blood:	Gold	Green and blue	Red
Thread:	White (silver)	Black	Red
Wisdom:	Spirit gnosis	Ordeal	Ancestor
Knowledge:	Spirit knowledge	Earned knowledge	Passed knowledge
Well:	Well of Wyrd (Urd)	Seething Cauldron (Nidhogg)	Well of Wisdom (Mimir)
Magick:	Power	Money	Sex
	Blessing/cursing	Prosperity	Love, lust
	Protection/attack	Fertility of land	Fertility of people
Art:	Alchemy	Medicine, agriculture	Anatomy
Profession:	Blacksmith	Herbalism, farming	Bone setting, husbandry

CHART 3: CORRESPONDENCES OF THE RAYS

The fourth ray is associated with green, which easily gives it an association with the second ray, dealing with love and nature. We can see this energy as a manifested expression of the second ray in the material world and among humans. It is really a mix of blue and yellow, or love and wisdom.

The fifth ray is based on the color orange and the Qabalistic qualities of orange, including science, technology, information, and communication. All of these disciplines fall under the Qabalistic sephira of Hod, or splendor. Orange is a mix of red and yellow, or will and wisdom. It is the knowledge of humanity, but not elevated to the heights described in the primary third ray. It is knowledge applied.

The sixth ray is indigo, a deep blue bordering on purple. It is a mix of blue and red, or of love and will. Theosophically, it is associated with religious devotion and philosophical education.

The seventh ray is violet and is said to be the ray for the new aeon, the ray of magick, ceremony, and alchemy. Though violet truly is a mix of blue and red, from our magickal perspective the violet ray often is described as being tinted with metallic gold or silver, and we can consider the intersection of all three primary rays—red, blue and yellow—to create the dazzling violet color of this ray. The seventh ray is the ray of the New Age because we must unite our power, love, and wisdom to truly manifest its power.

The Triune Power and Ninefold Nature of Reality

From the Great Two Powers always comes a mediating force.
From Energy and Matter comes the Cosmic Egg of Creation.
From the Darkness and the Light comes the Twilight.
From the Goddess and the God comes the Child of Promise.

Three Occurs in Space: Above, Below, and Between.
These are the realms of the Great Witch Tree,
The World Tree that grows through Three Rings and Nine Worlds,
The Tree of Life around which all the universe revolves.

These are the realms of the Starry Heavens.
Here everything is eternal.
Here everything is perfect.
Here nothing changes.
All is Bornless.

These are the realms of the Fertile Earth.
Here everything changes.

Here is the flow of flux and reflux.
Here nothing stays the same.
All is Ever Changing.

These are the realms of the Chthonic Underworld.
Here things grow in the darkness.
Here reflections are seen.
Here you face the shadow.
All is found and all is lost.

Three Occurs in Time: Past, Present, and Future.
They are the Moirae, the Parcae, the Norns, and the Wyrd Sisters.
They are the Apportioners, the Sparring Ones, Dame Fata.

They are known as Urd, She who is of the past.
She who is Clotho, the spinner who has spun the thread of life from her distaff.
She is Nona, the Ninth, who spun the thread to her spindle and summoned upon
* ninth month of birth.*

They are known as Verdandi, She who is becoming.
She is Lachesis, who measures the thread of life on her rod .
She is Decima, the Tenth, who weaves life into being and draws the lots of life.

They are known as Skuld, She who is obligated to be.
She is Atropos, the inexorable cutter of the thread of life with her abhorred shears.
She is Morta, Death who chooses the time of our ending.

They are the never ending, ever turning Ladies of Fate.

Three Occur in Energy: Will, Love, and Wisdom.
By a Straight Line is the Angelic Fire.
By a Bent Line is the Faery Flame.
By a Crooked Line is the Witch Fire of Cunning and Wisdom.

Together, they create the ninefold plot of creation.
Three Rays radiate out from the Source.
Three Worlds receive them.
Three Times manifest them.

PART TWO:
POWER OF THE THREE RAYS

CHAPTER FOUR:
INNER ALCHEMY

What then is the root of poetry and every other wisdom? Not hard;
three cauldrons are born in every person. —"The Cauldron of Poesy"

Alchemy is a term that is shrouded in both mystery and misunderstanding. The origin of the term is debated by scholars, likely meaning "the art of transformation," and has links to both Arabic and Greek. Occult tradition tells us the word comes from Egypt, known as the land of Khemet by the ancient Egyptians, from the word *khem*, referring to black fertile sand, not barren desert sand. Egypt was known as the land of the black sand, the fertile soil that washes down the Nile.

While we might think of its root in Egypt, alchemy in various forms was practiced in both the East and West, including China, Persia, India, Greece, and even as far as Spain, and eventually the image of the alchemist evolved into the popular one we have of a wizard-like figure in the laboratory, mixing chemicals in an effort to change lead into gold. While there is truth to that image, it also is the source of great misunderstanding, as people then and now believed alchemy was a scheme to get rich by attaining precious metals. Later it was said that alchemical teachings were wrong, and alchemy's poetic teachings on the structure of matter eventually led to the rise of modern chemistry and the Periodic Table of the Elements rather than the alchemist's four "elements" of fire, air, water, and earth.

Alchemy truly is an art, science, and spiritual discipline of transformation, and the transmutation of lead into gold was only one application, an outer manifestation of an inner experience. It was believed that the alchemist invoked a different set of principles to govern the world, including, but going beyond, those we understand through modern chemistry. Those of an appropriate level of spiritual growth will be capable of feats of which non-alchemists will not. Bending reality is a common theme in many traditions, as the miracles, magick, and psychic powers of these highly developed spiritual masters seem impossible feats to ordinary people. In terms of laboratory experiments, the idea that an individual alchemist can affect the outcome of the experiment differently than someone else echoes poetically some of our modern teachings on quantum physics, such as that the observer in an experiment can affect the outcome of the experiment. The scientist and the observer are not independent and separate but are part of a greater system, a greater whole.

If the alchemist had not undergone the appropriate inner transformations, then he or she would not be able to transform the lead into gold. Transmutation is both a test and a journey of discovery, and the great teacher on the journey is Mother Nature, along with her plants, minerals, and metals. She is the first and foremost alchemist. By studying her, we, too, can become alchemists. Changing lead into gold is also an allegory for enlightenment. The dense "lead" of unwanted energies, no matter if the energies are called sin in the Christian tradition or karma in the East, must be transformed into the pure, incorruptible "gold." This transformation also is known as finding the Philosopher's Stone, either a literal or a metaphoric stone or elixir that grants immortality, total health, and wisdom.

Alchemy is not a religion, but rather is an occult science that blends well with the esoteric aspects of any tradition. It has been associated with pagan traditions as well as Jewish, Christian, and Islamic faiths, and our popular European traditions of alchemy are colorful amalgamations of all these encoded in secret symbols, ciphers, and imagery easily misunderstood by others. Today, alchemy generally is considered a Hermetic tradition, relating to the overall body of lore associated with the figure of Hermes Trismegistus, who is strongly linked to the Egyptian Thoth, arguably the first mythical alchemist. While we tend to think of alchemy as primarily a set of external practices, many traditions of alchemy, particularly those that survive in the East, emphasize the internal practices. Though Western psychology has adopted alchemical words and ideas, the internal practice of alchemy is not simply a form of psychology but is an esoteric system of transformation based on the movement of energy within the body. All of these currents of alchemical thought have gone on to influence modern alchemists, ritual magicians, esoteric healers, and modern Witches.

The vision of the three rays of Witchcraft has added to my own insight into alchemy and how these powerful forces can be applied within the body and in our relationship with Mother Nature, truly the first alchemist.

Such alchemical energy work helps us reconnect the various parts of ourselves that are disconnected. As with tubing, pipes, and laboratory beakers, if there is no connection between vessels, then there can be no flow, no distillation, and no receptacle to contain and use the power. The essence of the three rays vision is one of connectivity. All of us have our part to play in creation, and that creation is renewed when all parts are understood and connected, allowing the integration of power, love, and wisdom in all things. Connecting the parts of the inner self mirrors the connection we forge in the outer world. One of the basic maxims of magick is "As above, so below." We must make the changes we desire internally, in our consciousness and our own energy systems, before we can ever manifest them on the outer, material planes.

You cannot connect all the parts of your inner self if you do not know exactly what parts are there to connect. Spiritual anatomy, while very real, seems to offer a more subjective experience than physical anatomy. Each tradition of alchemy and esoteric healing has its own view of the spiritual anatomy. All seem to work within the context of their tradition, and even have parallels with other systems, yet they are not as objective as the medical examiner's description of our bodily organs and systems. Operating on a higher plane of development, our spiritual organs are not as manifest as our bodily organs, and there is always a measure of creativity in their description. The systems of Chinese traditional medicine and acupuncture differ greatly from Tibetan traditional medicine and Hindu ayurvedic medicine, and even more so from Qabalistic Hermetic magick, yet all seem to work for their clients and practitioners. Each describes similar points of energy and the lines that connect them, but the maps look quite different.

I believe our energy systems are much like music, as both subtle energy and music are based on vibration. Our individual energy is like a long string, or several strings, running vertically through the body. Many traditions look at energy points—popularly called *chakras*, borrowing from the Hindu traditions—along the main axis of the body. The most popular chakra system has seven points, from the base of the spine to the crown of the head, and modern teachings relate them to the colors of the rainbow. This line from the root to the crown is like a string found on a guitar or violin. The chakras are like the standard Western musical scale of seven notes. Most people in the West are used to listening to music composed in this pattern, and are familiar with the scale using the words Do-Re-Mi-Fa-So-La-Ti and repeating the first note in the higher octave, Do.

Western music actually is based on a twelve-tone system of notes. The seven-note scale used in the example would be the familiar white keys on a piano. The additional five notes to make a total of twelve are the black keys on the piano. Some modern esoteric forms of healing have extended the chakra system from seven chakras to twelve, much like this scale. Other cultures use other tonal systems, which often sound "alien" to Western ears. Forms of tribal music, as well as the music indigenous to the Middle East, often use quarter-tone measurements, splitting the Western semitone into two separate notes, as well as other micro-tonal measurements that are almost too subtle for the traditional Western listener. Western composers experimented with these measurements in the nineteenth century, but they did not become popular enough to be familiar to most listeners.

What does a discussion of musical tones have to do with the energy system of the body? Each system, each ritual, and each meditation is like playing a piece of music. Your experience of the subtle energy system can be as complex or as simple as the energetic "scale" you are using. We all are playing in the same range of energy, the energy found in and around the human body, but each of us is working in a different "scale" or different system, providing different qualities, experiences, and results but all arguably working with the same fundamental forces. This validates most systems of internal energy work, and gives us the freedom to try different systems and experiment in a safe and balanced manner.

For the purpose of the three rays of Witchcraft work, I'm going to keep things as simple as possible, staying in the motif of three. Think of it as a musical scale with only three notes, like you are pressing the string down in only three places to create your notes.

While we have intricate systems of energy points and spiritual anatomy in the East, and even in the Qabalistic Hermetic systems of the West, the inspiration for much of the rays of Witchcraft is pagan European, and Celtic specifically. Sadly, we don't know if the Celts had their own intricate systems of energy points and soul anatomy.

The practitioners of the true Druidic tradition of the Celts generally did not write things down, working instead from an oral tradition, and with their destruction first at the hands of the Romans and then later in the Christian era, we have very little true knowledge of what they believed, practiced, or taught. Much of our current spiritual information on the Celts comes from the efforts of Celtic reconstructionists relying on archaeological evidence, surviving folklore, and what was written down about the Celts and their myths during the early Christian era, most notably by Christian monks. Modern Witches with a spiritual or ancestral connection to the Celts have used this information to inspire them in their own practices.

One intriguing piece of "evidence" adopted by many modern practitioners comes from the "Cauldron of Poesy," a sixteenth-century poem from the Irish fili, the poet-mystics (legal codex H.3.18, dated to c. 1500 CE). Though translations are found from more traditional Celtic scholars, it was first brought to the attention of the occult world by both Caitlin Matthews and Erynn Rowan Laurie, also known as Erynn Darkstar.

The "Cauldron of Poesy" text could possibly refer to a secret teaching on a series of three energetic points, like chakras, described as cauldrons within the body by the Irish fili. This makes an interesting connection to the forms of Eastern inner alchemy lore, as the various points often are described in terms of vessels, containers, and equipment, such as the "triple warmer" and the "governing vessel." In the "Cauldron of Poesy," each person is said to be born with three cauldrons within the body (chart 4), yet each person does not get the same amount of "fluid" in each cauldron. Discrepancies in the amount of fluid apportioned by the gods in each person can grant either no knowledge, little knowledge, or great knowledge and inspiration.

Cauldron	Name	Condition	Location	Purpose
Lower	Incubation	Upright	Belly	Survival, life needs
Middle	Motion	Tipped	Heart	Emotion, poetic urge
Upper	Wisdom	Overturned	Head	True wisdom, magick

CHART 4: THE THREE CAULDRONS

The lower cauldron, found in the belly, is the Cauldron of Incubation, or what I term the Cauldron of Life. It is the only cauldron that is fully active in everyone, as it appears upright and contains the energy of survival, or basic life force. This is what powers our body and basic needs. In our three rays vision, it resonates most strongly with the energies of the first ray, the ray of will and power. It embodies the most basic form of will, the will to survive.

The middle cauldron is the Cauldron of Motion, though I sometimes refer to it simply as the Cauldron of the Heart, for it is envisioned in the chest. This unusual cauldron is said to be tipped on its side in most people, neither up nor down. This might be similar to modern healers referring to the heart chakra as being blocked. In the text, this cauldron is said to be turned by either sorrow or joy, meaning intense emotions can turn the cauldron upright and prepare it for the process to be filled. In broader terms, the joy and sorrow of the heart are forms of emotional expansion and contraction that work together to align the Cauldron of the Heart.

Sorrow is defined as longing, grief, jealousy, and, strangely, discipline, which could be considered a form of restriction and thus sorrow. Joy is divided into divine joy and human joy, with human joy consisting of a variety of human experiences including sexual intimacy, health untroubled, the wisdom of good poetry, and the poetic frenzy inspired by the magickal hazel nuts. Once turned upright, the Cauldron of Motion allows the free flow of emotion and, on a higher level, contains the poetic urge and creative drive. Those who embody the powers of the Cauldron of Motion are granted nine abilities or virtues from the cauldron, listed as follows: Bestows, Extends, Nourishes, Magnifies, Invokes, Sings, Preserves, Arranges, and Supports. From the perspective of our three rays, this cauldron embodies the second ray, the ray of love.

The highest cauldron is called the Cauldron of Wisdom, located in the skull. It is said to be turned down in all people except the most inspired and wise. It is the center of true wisdom and magickal power, not just knowledge or emotion. It is the vessel that is filled with the flowing power of awen. Its fires are what illuminate the skull when the poet experiences "fire in the head."

The three cauldrons fit together quite well with other Witchcraft teachings. Those who claim descent from a pre-Gardnerian Craft often teach about three power points within the body that have different associations and colors as compared to the chakras, but which line up quite well with the belly, heart, and head chakras. The concept of inner cauldrons also parallels teachings found in Eastern Taoist alchemy, where inner transformations with life force and bodily fluids are the tools of the alchemist.

The cauldron teaching also fits in well with the recently more popular notion of the triune soul, found in more shamanic and ecstatic branches of Witchcraft. Drawing from such varied sources as Hawaiian Huna, Voodou, Siberian shamanism, Egyptian magick, and European folklore, and making its way into modern Craft traditions such as the Anderson Feri line, the Reclaiming tradition, and the Temple of Witchcraft tradition, the basic premise of this teaching is that we are not single-souled individuals but rather are many-souled. We have a body that has its own life essence, its own body consciousness, and many of our traits from this lifetime that are not eternal are tied to the body. This body is known as the middle self, or middle soul, for it is oriented primarily toward the Middle World. We also have a soul that is impersonal, that sees the big picture and is concerned primarily with the heavens. It is known as the higher self, or higher soul. Lastly, we have an instinctive or intuitive soul, alternatively described as childlike and playful, or animalistic. Though it acts as a messenger between the higher and middle selves, its nature orients it with the Underworld.

Many different traditions have similar soul concepts and different names for the three selves (chart 5). Most of these cultures and traditions have more than three parts to the self and, much like energy systems, divide the whole in different ways, making it difficult to match similar terms with the exact same definitions.

We find the same triple nature of the soul in alchemy. Alchemists refer to sulfur, mercury, and salt. While these three names sometimes refer to chemicals, more often they are poetic ciphers, codes describing primal forces. In the universe,

Tradition	Higher Self	Middle Self	Lower Self
Alchemy	Sulfur	Salt	Mercury
Anglo-Saxon	Mód	Myne (Memory/Emotion), Hyge (Intellect), Lic (Body)	Fetch
Arabic	Sirr	Ruch	Noph
Celtic	Enaid	Féin	Púca or Scal
Egyptian	Sa (Ba)	Ba (Sa)	Ka
English	Soul	Body	Spirit
Greek/Roman	Logos, Daimon	Thumo	Epithymia, Psyche
Hawaiian	Aumakua	Uhane	Unihipili
Hebrew	Neshamah	Ruach	Nephesh
Latin	Anima	Corpus	Spiritus
Norse	Sal	Sjalfr (Personal Self), Lík/Lyke (Body)	Fylgja/Fetch
Siberian	Ami	Suld	Suns
Taoist	Hun	—	P'o
Voodou	Gros bon ange	N'ame	Petit bon ange
Temple of Witchcraft	Watcher	Namer	Shaper
Inner Temple of Witchcraft	Divine Mind	Personal Mind	Psychic Mind
African Feri	Ori	Emi	Vivi
Cora Anderson Feri	Gamma	Beta	Alpha
Victor Anderson Feri	God Self	Human Self	Animal Self
Morningstar Feri	Sacred Dove	Shining Body	Sticky One
Blue Rose Feri	Holy Daimon	Talker	Fetch
Starhawk Reclaiming	Deep Self	Talking Self	Younger Self
Orion Foxwood Faery	Star Walker	Surface Walker	Dream Walker
Serge Kahili King Huna	Kane	Lono	Ku

CHART 5: THE THREE SELVES

they are the creative, dissolving, and sustaining forces. In human consciousness, they are the soul, spirit, and body. Everything manifested in the universe has this triune nature, but in humanity it could be called soul, body, and spirit, viewing the spirit and soul as two distinct components while most modern thought sees them as the same. Medieval occultists also looked at the world as having a triune nature, with the terms Anima Mundi, or soul of the world, which would be the equivalent of Mother Nature; the Spiritus Mundi, the spirit or life energy of the world; and the Corpus Mundi, the body of the planet itself, including the land, minerals, plants, and even animals.

The three-soul model fits into our bodily cauldrons with ease. The lower Cauldron of Life deals with basic life instincts and needs, much as the lower self does. Such operations occur intuitively. We don't put conscious thought into the heart beating, the blood pumping, digestion, or basic breathing. They are automatic and instinctual. The middle Cauldron of the Heart deals with human life, joy, and sorrow and the experiences we have in relationship, making it the perfect match for the very human middle self, which contains our ego, our personality, and the connections of our relationships. The highest cauldron, the Cauldron of Wisdom, deals with magick and true spiritual insight, much like the higher self looking down from a heavenly perspective, providing the flow of awen to the middle self.

The initiations of magickal traditions, formalized in ritual or as the ordeals of life, appear to tip and fill these cauldrons with power. Our regular practices maintain the flow between the cauldrons, just as a yogi's work maintains the flow of energy between the chakras. But it takes a mystery experience to tip the cauldron right-side up, just as in traditional Hindu mysticism it often takes the touch and initiation of a master to truly open and enliven a chakra center.

Though the mysteries of traditional degrees are divided differently in various traditions, they can be seen in three basic forms, also corresponding to the cauldrons within us. Basically they consist of an awakening experience, often an awakening to power, magick, or psychic ability. In traditional initiations, this is the declaration to become a Witch, with some ritual having you face a mirror and declare yourself a Witch in the sacred circle, with the approval of your elders. The second mystery revolves around death and rebirth, particularly through the rituals of the Descent of the Goddess. You must face the powers of the Underworld with all their shadows, and be reborn. This is akin to the sorrow and subsequent divine joy that can occur in the Cauldron of the Heart. The third mystery, granting the status of full clergy in the form of High Priestess or High Priest, is sexual in nature. Though sexual intimacy is a trigger for turning the Cauldron of the Heart, it is not just sexual intimacy between humans in this mystery but is the divine union between us and the gods, often embodied in the ritual of the Great Rite. During this ritual, which is done symbolically with the blade and chalice or sexually, the Priest invokes the God and the Priestess invokes the Goddess, and with these divine unions in the physical body of the Witches, the union is consummated. It is in essence the power of creation that comes with godhood, most appropriate for the third cauldron. In this ritual, the secret names of the gods, the hidden knowledge, are passed on.

In my own experiences with the three rays, I have developed a system of inner alchemy that is reminiscent of Taoist alchemical exercises I've learned. Each of the cauldrons "brews" a different vital life force, processing a power within us but also connecting us to the worlds around us, expanding our consciousness.

In these workings, the lower Cauldron of Life is used to brew together the four elements, the essence of the world and life as manifest through the powers of fire, air, water, and earth. The four elements are found in a variety of esoteric systems, providing a foundation in alchemy. They are also a fundamental concept in modern Witchcraft, used in the Witch's circle, as the entities that rule the elements are used as guardians and helpers from the four directions. Earth rules issues of the material realm, home, and finance. Water rules issues of relationships, emotions, and love. Air rules issues of ideas, communication, and memory. Fire rules issues of passion, desire, and energy. Through their alchemical fusion, they develop the fifth element, the quintessence of alchemists, from which all things emanate and to which all things will return. Modern Witches call the fifth element *spirit*, and designate the top point of the pentacle for this element (figure 7).

The middle Cauldron of the Heart raises the terrestrial energies of the lower cauldron and mingles them with the powers emanating in the solar world, the

FIGURE 7: PENTACLE

planets that are in their own way like the chakras or cauldrons of the solar system, the solar being. Here we brew a more refined power of the Sun, Moon, Mercury, Venus, Mars, Jupiter, and Saturn. The seven planets and their associated metals often are equated with the chakra systems familiar to most modern metaphysical practitioners (chart 6). These planets represent a range of evolution in consciousness. The planetary forces work together and become refined until they, too, reach up and resonate with the stars.

Chakra	Planet	Metal	Operation	Key Words
Crown	Sun	Gold	Conjunction	Self, identity, illumination
Brow	Moon	Silver	Distillation	Vision, sight, psychic
Throat	Mercury	Quicksilver	Fermentation	Communication, thought
Heart	Venus	Copper	Coagulation	Love, connection, empathy
Solar Plexus	Mars	Iron	Separation	Will, force, power
Belly	Jupiter	Tin	Dissolution	Expansion, trust
Root	Saturn	Lead	Calcination	Karma, lessons, grounding

CHART 6: CHAKRA CORRESPONDENCES

The work of the upper cauldron, the Cauldron of Wisdom, is to gather this starry wisdom. We gather the energy of the three rays of awen and brew our own greal, our own potion of inspiration, within the cauldron of the skull. This could be an allegory for hormonal processes occurring in the brain, but also for conferring wisdom and magickal power akin to that of the bards, magicians, and Witches of ages past. We must gather the light of the stars, going beyond our planet, our solar system, to the furthest reaches, for that is what is in alignment with the highest self. In one of the classic poems of the *Hanes Taliesin*, the bard Taliesin, or someone writing under his magickal name, tells us, "And my original country is the region of the summer stars." This echoes the sentiment in the Orphic Mysteries of the Greeks, saying, "I am a child of Earth and starry Heaven; But my race is of Heaven (alone). This ye know yourselves." Even our modern scholars know this to be true, with Dr. Carl Sagan exclaiming, "We are star-stuff," as we explore the universe with science. It is to that star-stuff that we will return, but rather than leave and go out or away from the world, we are called to bring it down into material form, manifesting the highest of these powers within the body. The three powers descend from the heavens as inspiration and first enter the cauldron of the skull before descending to the other cauldrons or circulating through the body and aura. All our work with the elements and planets is done to prepare us to be the vessel for this new light upon Earth.

We perceive this flow of the three rays coming both from the cauldron in the center of Annwn and from the stars, revealing a fundamental paradox in the mysteries. The light originates from both the stars and the darkness. The sources of the Underworld and Upper World are each other, creating a loop of infinity. Those who reach the highest of the heavens and the further reaches of outer space end up in the heart of the Underworld. Why do you think the sky is so dark at night? Those who descend into the furthest depths find the stars within the Earth, and find themselves in space, in the heavens. The Cauldron of Creation in Annwn is surrounded by these stars in Gwynvyd and also contains the stars within itself. The stars radiate the light of the three rays.

First Cauldron Working:
Synthesis of the Elements

The purpose of the first cauldron working is to prepare the body by uniting the four elements of earth, air, fire, and water. Greater mastery over the four elements, and ultimately their synthesis, is the foundational stone of many magickal traditions, preparing you for deeper and more transformative work.

Reach down to the heart of the planet Earth with your will, love, and wisdom, engaging the entire self. Draw down into the depths of the Earth, to the primordial garden where the patterns of the Earth are unspoiled by humanity. Beyond the heart of the Earth lie the Underworld, the deep of Annwn, and the Cauldron of Creation. Here we call the four elements, seeking to reconnect to that first pattern.

By light,
I invoke the power of fire,
Primordial starfire that burns in the heart of all matter.
I call to you that embodies passion and drive.
I call to you that embodies desire and will.
I call to you, keeper of divine victory.
The spear in the hand of every master.

Draw up the power of fire from the heart of the Earth, through your body and into your belly, into the Cauldron of Life. Feel the "fuel" beneath the first cauldron spark and ignite into flames, heating the liquid life force of the cauldron. Feel the fire reach around the edges of this belly cauldron and enter into the cauldron, immersing itself in the liquid life force, but not be extinguished. Feel your belly fill with fire, the power of passion, of will and vitality.

By life,
I invoke the power of air,
First breath of the gods animating all things.
I call to you that embodies awareness and perception.
I call to you that embodies memory and language.
I call to you, keeper of divine truth.
The sword in the hand of every master.

Draw up the power of air from the heart of the Earth, through your body and into the belly, into the Cauldron of Life. Feel the air feed the flames of the cauldron, making the fire beneath grow brighter. Feel the air reach up and over the lip of the cauldron, immersing itself in the liquid life force. Feel your belly fill with air, the power of the mind, of communication and truth.

By love,
I invoke the power of water,
Ancient womb that is the source of all births in the world.
I call to you that embodies emotion and relationships.
I call to you that embodies feelings and sentiment.
I call to you, keeper of divine compassion.
The grail in the hand of every master.

Draw up the power of water from the heart of the Earth, through your body and into the belly, into the Cauldron of Life. Feel the water reach up and over the lip of the cauldron, filling the cauldron, adding to the mix of life force. Feel your belly fill with water, with the power of emotion, relationships, and compassion.

By law,
I invoke the power of earth,
Original form to the world we know.
I call to you that embodies form and shape.
I call to you that embodies home and resource.
I call to you, keeper of divine sovereignty.
The stone upon which every master stands.

Draw up the power of earth from the heart of the Earth, through your body and into the belly, into the Cauldron of Life. Feel the earth energy reach up over the lip of the cauldron and fill it to the brim, adding to the potent mix of life force. Feel your belly fill with earth, with the power of form, resources, and sovereignty.

By liberty,
I conjure the power of spirit,
Quintessence, akasha, ether.
I call to you, first and last of the elements.
I call to you, alpha and omega of creation.
The crown of stars and stones,
The crown of humility upon the head of every master.

Feel the four elements mix with your vital life force in the cauldron. These four powers—energy, thought, feeling, and structure—are the basic components of life. Feel the four streams of elemental energy continue to rise from the depths and feed your cauldron. Feel as the four streams of elemental light mix together and form a beam of brilliant, multicolored light. Feel the four energies fuse together, becoming stronger than their individual parts, becoming the pure, refined essence of the fifth element, of spirit, the source of the First Matter and the One Thing, the essence of our unformed Philosopher's Stone.

Feel this power flow out of your belly cauldron and circulate throughout the body. Feel the energy flow to wherever your body needs it, wherever you are in need of healing. Feel it rise and ignite the fires of the Cauldron of the Heart in the chest and the Cauldron of Wisdom in the head. Feel it fill the Cauldron of the Heart with elemental life force. Feel the heart's power rise, as it becomes steam, rising to the head. Feel the steam gather and condense inside the Cauldron of Wisdom. Feel its power increase as the cauldron begins to fill. Feel the life force rise out of the crown and flow down your body, as if your spine were a fountain and the cauldrons were tiered basins on the fountain, gathering this elemental life force. Feel it fill your entire being, the energy field around you known as the aura. You are infused with vital life force. You are blessed with the gifts of the Cauldron of Life.

Second Cauldron Working:
Embodying the Seven Wanderers

Bring all your awareness to the heart space, to the Cauldron of the Heart. Reach into your own heart with your will, love, and wisdom. Feel the heart. Evaluate the heart. Is it open or closed? Is the cauldron upright or tipped? Are you able to retain within it the essence of love, which is the power of motion, or does the life force of the elements from the Cauldron of Life below simply pass through it?

Remember your sorrows and joys. Think of the times when your heart has contracted or expanded. This motion of expansion and contraction tips the cauldron and gives it the potential for power. If you feel your cauldron is not fully upright, but is tipped over or on its side, then think about your sorrows and joys. Feel your sorrows and joys.

Feel your longing, your losses that you mourn. Feel your jealousy. Feel all the aches in your heart. Remember the times you have been restricted and could not do what you wanted to do but had to do what you must.

Feel your joys, your passions and sexual intimacy. Feel the health within your body or, if unhealthy, when you have been healthy in the past. Think of the art, music, and poetry that have inspired you. What did you feel then?

Alternate your remembrances between sorrow and joy until you feel an awakening in the heart, until you feel your will, love, and wisdom open the cauldron and turn it upright within you.

Feel the star awaken within the Cauldron of the Heart. It is like the Sun within. Just as the Sun is the center of our solar system and the other planets revolve around it, the Sun within calls out to the planetary energies and orders them in the pattern of the macrocosm. Call for the wandering stars and empower the heart.

I call forth the power of Saturn, Harsh Teacher and Constrictor.

Feel the black light of the dark, wandering star of Saturn enter your heart. It might simply enter from the world around you, descend from the heavens through the crown and into your heart, or rise from below and into your heart. Feel the power of the Taskmaster, embodied in the Underworld King or Dark Crone and Queen of the Dead.

I call forth the power of Jupiter, Gentle Teacher and Expander.

Feel the blue light of the benevolent giant wanderer Jupiter enter your heart. As with Saturn, the light might come from between, above, or below to enter your heart. Feel the power of the Gentle Teacher, embodied by the Sky Father or Storm King.

I call forth the power of Mars, Warrior-Protector.

Feel the red light of the warrior star Mars enter your heart from between, above, or below. Feel the power of the War God.

I call forth the power of Venus, Enchantress and Lover.

Feel the green light of the wandering beauty Venus enter your heart from between, above, or below. Feel the power of the Enchantress, embodied by the Goddess of Love or a beautiful maiden.

I call forth the power of Mercury, Messenger and Magician.

Feel the orange or silver light of the messenger Mercury enter your heart from between, above, or below. Feel the power of the Messenger, embodied by a magician, elder, or youth.

I call forth the power of Luna, Queen of Heaven and Earth.

Feel the silver-white light of the Moon enter your heart from between, above, or below. Feel the power of the Moon Goddess, embodied as the crescent-crowned Queen.

I call forth the power of the Sol, King of Stars and Child of Light.

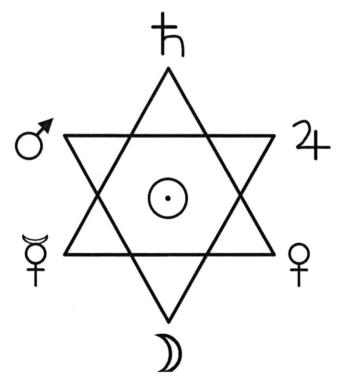

FIGURE 8: HEXAGRAM

Feel the golden light of the Sun enter your heart from between, above, or below. Feel the power of the Sun King, embodied as the Regal Lord or Child of Light.

Feel the six planetary powers gather around the Sun in the center, forming a hexagram, a six-pointed star, of light (figure 8). Feel the seven individual points become like one in the star of the hexagram. Feel them become a heavenly star within your heart. Feel the powers of the cosmos radiating forth from your heart, your cauldron. Feel this heart star's light touch your head and shine out from your crown and your eyes. Feel its light descend into the belly. Feel the light, heat, gravity, and power of this heart star shine forth into every cell and then shine out as if each cell was a lens, magnifying the power and radiating it to all with whom you have contact.

Third Cauldron Working:
Invocation of the Three Rays

Reach up to the heavens with your will, love, and wisdom, and draw down the three rays of Witchcraft. Call down the first ray with this invocation:

By the straight line,
I invoke the first ray.
I invoke the red ray.
I invoke the unbending ray of cold red archangelic flame.
I invoke the ray of will and power.

Pull down the energy of the first ray. Ask yourself, "What is the will of the heavens?" Listen. Feel. Then say, "I enact the will of the heavens." This connection to heavenly will then helps open the powers of the first ray to descend safely into your body and three cauldrons.

Feel the first ray descend and enter your head, burning with a red flame. Ask yourself, "What is the will of the head?" Listen. Feel. Then say, "I enact the will of the head."

Feel as if the upper cauldron is filled to the brim with the first ray of inspiration, which spills over, draining down into the chest, to the heart. Feel the first ray descend from the head into the heart, now burning with a golden flame. Ask yourself, "What is the will of the heart?" Listen. Feel. Then say, "I enact the will of the heart."

Feel the heart fill up with this energy, which again spills over, down into the Cauldron of Life in the belly. Feel the power of the first ray descend from the heart into the belly, now burning with a white flame. Ask yourself, "What is the will of the body?" Listen. Feel. Then say, "I enact the will of the body."

Feel the Cauldron of Life also fill up with energy, which spills over, as the flowing energy connects you to the Earth and down below it, to the Underworld. Ask yourself, "What is the will of the Earth and Underworld?" Listen. Feel. Then say, "I enact the will of the Earth and Underworld."

Say: "There are no limits to my power. All is possible."

Call down the second ray with this invocation:

By the bent line,
I invoke the second ray.
I invoke the blue ray.
I invoke the spiraling ray of electric blue faery flame.
I invoke the ray of love and trust.

Pull down the energy of the second ray. Ask yourself, "What is the love of the heavens?" Listen. Feel. Then say, "I feel the love of the heavens." This connection to heavenly will then helps open the powers of the second ray to descend safely into your body and three cauldrons.

Feel the second ray descend and enter your head, burning with a blue flame. Ask yourself, "What is the love of the head?" Listen. Feel. Then say, "I feel the love of the head."

Feel as if the upper cauldron is filled to the brim with the second ray of inspiration, which spills over, draining down into the chest, to the heart. Feel the second ray descend from the head into the heart, now burning with a green flame. Ask yourself, "What is the love of the heart?" Listen. Feel. Then say, "I feel the love of the heart."

Feel the heart fill up with this energy, which again spills over, down into the Cauldron of Life in the belly. Feel the power of the second ray descend from the heart into the belly, now burning with a black flame. Ask yourself, "What is the love of the body?" Listen. Feel. Then say, "I feel the love of the body."

Feel the Cauldron of Life also fill up with energy, which spills over, as the flowing energy connects you to the Earth and down below it, to the Underworld. Ask yourself, "What is the love of the Earth and Underworld?" Listen. Feel. Then say, "I feel the love of the Earth and Underworld."

Say, "There are no limits to my love. All is one."

Call down the third ray with this invocation:

By the crooked line,
I invoke the third ray.
I invoke the yellow ray.
I invoke the crooked ray of serpentine gold Witch fire.
I invoke the ray of wisdom and cunning.

Pull down the energy of the third ray. Ask yourself, "What is the wisdom of the heavens?" Listen. Feel. Then say, "I know the wisdom of the heavens." This connection to heavenly will then helps open the powers of the third ray to descend safely into your body and three cauldrons.

Feel the third ray descend and enter your head, burning with a yellow flame. Ask yourself, "What is the wisdom of the head?" Listen. Feel. Then say, "I know the wisdom of the head."

Feel as if the upper cauldron is filled to the brim with the first ray of inspiration, which spills over, draining down into the chest, to the heart. Feel the third ray descend from the head into the heart, now burning with a red flame. Ask yourself, "What is the wisdom of the heart?" Listen. Feel. Then say, "I know the wisdom of the heart."

Feel the heart fill up with this energy, which again spills over, down into the Cauldron of Life in the belly. Feel the power of the third ray descend from the heart into the belly, now burning with a scarlet flame. Ask yourself, "What is the wisdom of the body?" Listen. Feel. Then say, "I know the wisdom of the body."

Feel the Cauldron of Life also fill up with energy, which spills over, as the flowing energy connects you to the Earth and down below it, to the Underworld. Ask yourself, "What is the wisdom of the Earth and Underworld?" Listen. Feel. Then say, "I know the wisdom of the Earth and Underworld."

Say, "There are no limits to my wisdom. All is known."

CHAPTER FIVE:
OUTER ALLIES—
THE THREE RACES

*These siths (people of the Sidhe) . . . are said to be of a middle
nature (halfway) betwixt man and Angel, as were daemons
thought to be of old. —The Secret Commonwealth of Elves, Fauns
and Fairies by Robert Kirk*

The three rays of Witchcraft depict three evolutionary streams of life not considered in our traditional models of scientific evolution. Just as physical cellular life
theoretically began with one common single-celled ancestor, the First Mother, and
eventually branched off into the myriad plant, animal, and fungal life we have now
on planet Earth, so has our common spiritual source, our common ancestor from
the cauldron, which we may think of as the Creator in its many forms, branched
off into several separate and distinct streams of spiritual life.

One of the problems with our current human-centric view is the idea of a
ladder of evolution, where an entity, physical or spiritual, is above or below us.
While we fancy ourselves to be the height of animal evolution, or even planetary
evolution, we still tend to look at ourselves as above or below the variety of spirits
from our mythologies and religions. We want to know where we rank. While
this model of vertical hierarchy might have been appropriate for the previous
ages, culminating with the teachings of Pisces, the vision proposed by the three

rays of Witchcraft is not one where we find our spiritual kin above or below us on a ladder, but where we find them next to us, standing side by side, with their own evolution and stream of life. While there may be special circumstances and connections between these streams of spirit life, one does not necessarily evolve into another. None is better or worse than the others. None is higher or lower. Each has its own unique blessings and challenges. Each needs the others for mutual survival and prosperity, just as animals and plants are in various reciprocal and even, in some cases, symbiotic relationships. The challenge is to maintain a symbiotic connection, where there is mutual exchange, rather than a parasitical relationship, where one is constantly taking from the other.

Those following the path of the Witch are challenged to build these reciprocal relationships with the other streams of life, not only to aid us as individuals but also to make connections that will aid the evolution of all the races. Not only do these beings become our spirit allies and helpers, but we must become theirs as well. Modern lore and teachings tend to stress what the spirits can do for us. They can help us manifest our desires, heal us, protect us, guide us, and teach us. Yet, to paraphrase a famous sacred king of the twentieth century, you must "ask not what the spirits can do for you, but ask what you can do for the spirits." They aid us in ways that are basically for our personal development, because it is their hope, in the multitude of humans they aid, that some will progress to a point of self-development where they then will look at the greater spiritual picture and realize aid must come from both sides. But it takes competent Witches, priestesses, magicians, and shamans to do this work for the spirit world. They aid us to get us to a minimum level of competency so we can develop more reciprocal relationships.

The Angelic Races

The first of the three races embodied by the glyph of the three rays is the angelic race. There is a wide range of conflicting lore regarding the form and nature of angels, dating back to the ancient pagan spirit hierarchies of Sumer, Babylon, Egypt, and Persia, to Jewish, Christian, and Islamic sources, and now a plethora of material in the modern metaphysical movement stemming from Hermetic, Spiritualist, Theosophical, and neopagan sources. Such sources list detailed hierarchies of different types of angels, each with separate forms and functions, yet few of them match.

Our earliest historical records of angels come from the Old Testament, depicting entities delivering messages for the God of the Old Testament or, in certain cases, enacting God's will, usually by destroying something. The word for angel is *mal'akh*, meaning "messenger." Other words associated with angels, such as *angelus* (Latin), *angelos* (Greek), *angaros* (Persian), and *angeres* (Sanskrit), have a similar meaning and give us versions of the more familiar name. They might be creatures from lore older than the Jewish Old Testament, with the possibility that such mythologies were adopted from Babylonian and Egyptian sources. Their mention in the Old Testament and later the Gospels and Qur'an has led to the development of complex mystical hierarchies by the esoteric practitioners of these religions, with little endorsement from the more exoteric religious authorities. Angels have become a matter of philosophical debate, with such questions as, "How many angels can dance on the head of a pin?"

From inspired teachings and visions reportedly based on the ancient mysteries, we are taught that angels embody a race of entities that have no free will. They are bound by the divine will of the Creator, and are set into motion to mediate aspects of creation. They have been described by some as cosmic bureaucrats, managing the universe and making sure everything that needs to function does indeed function. Their hierarchies are structured much like any corporation, neatly dividing duties, responsibilities, and functions, and making sure each manager has the necessary power and labor to fulfill those functions. Some angels rule over other orders, or "choirs," of angels, to ensure the job gets fulfilled. They take their orders from the top down, with the Creator as the chief executive officer in this cosmic boardroom.

Angels have no desire or will of their own, no creativity or personal drive, but rather seek to serve the will of the divine. In this regard, they fit the evolutionary stream of the first ray of will and power. This image can clash harshly with our modern idea of childlike cherubs and sentimental views of angelic love and kindness. I don't deny those experiences, but I do think they are sentimentalized. If an angel does a kind act, it is not out of the motivation of kindness and love. Such feelings are a byproduct. Its motivation is that such an act was within the will of the divine. We can easily mistake the connection and perfection of the divine as love, for love is one of the three main components of the divine, but the function of the angels is not to mediate the divine's love but to mediate the divine's will.

I also think that, with religious systems that allow a belief only in angels and look at many other spirits as automatically suspect and potentially evil, it's easy to mistake other spirit races that offer a pleasant experience for angels, leading to the popular notion that humans become angels upon death and protect us as guardian angels. While there is a lot of truth to the concepts of both ancestral and angelic guardians, they originate in two different streams of life.

Angels are divided into a variety of "races," each separate and distinct. While recent art tends to depict them in human terms—and, in fact, they are a race

Archangel	Archetype	Element	Direction	Planet(s)	Color(s)	Meaning of Name
Michael	Warrior	Fire	South	Sun/Mercury	Red, Yellow	He who is like God
Gabriel	Messenger	Water	West	Moon	Blue	God is my strength
Raphael	Physician	Air	East	Sun/Mercury	Yellow	God heals
Uriel	Teacher	Earth	North	Uranus	Green, black	Light of God
Chamuel	Justice	—	—	Mars	Red	He who sees God
Tzafkiel	Priestess	—	—	Saturn	Black	Contemplation of God
Tzadkiel	Priest	—	—	Jupiter	Blue	The righteousness of God
Haniel	Joy bringer	—	—	Venus	Green, pink	Grace of God
Raziel	Mystic	—	—	Zodiac	Gray	Secrets of God
Metatron	Chief	Spirit	Center	Stars	White	Serves the throne of God
Sandalphon	Guide	Earth	Center	Earth	Red, green, yellow, black	Brother, Co-Walker

CHART 7: ARCHANGELIC CORRESPONDENCES

without flesh, so they can take any shape desired and often do take human shapes to communicate—angels are depicted in more esoteric art as animalistic, transhuman, and even monstrous at times. While they can take on the appearance of being human, I think the more monstrous manifestations are to emphasize that these are nonhuman intelligences.

The two most common divisions of these entities are angels and archangels, usually with the connotation that the archangels are somehow superior to the regular angels. In the Jewish tradition, these groups usually number ten and often are considered "orders" associated with different points on the Tree of Life. The archangels are the "princes" of the orders, and each of the ten major archangels rules one order. In Christian traditions, the groups are called "choirs" and number nine in total. In this tradition, archangels are considered one of the lowest choirs, just above "angels," but play an important role in our development because they are so close to humanity.

Number	Sephira	Archangel	Angelic Order	Description
1	Kether	Metatron	Chaioth ha-Qadesh	Holy Living Creatures
2	Chokmah	Raziel	Auphanim	The Wheels
3	Binah	Tzafkiel	Aralim	The Mighty Ones, Thrones
4	Chesed	Tzadkiel	Chashmalim	The Shining/Brilliant Ones
5	Geburah	Chamuel	Seraphim	The Burning Ones
6	Tiphereth	Michael	Malakim	Kings
7	Netzach	Haniel	Elohim	Creative Ones/Gods
8	Hod	Raphael	Beni Elohim	Children of the Divine
9	Yesod	Gabriel	Kerubim	Strong Ones
10	Malkuth	Sandalphon	Ashim	Flames/Order of Blessed Souls

CHART 8: THE ANGELIC ORDERS OF THE TREE OF LIFE

In either system, the archangels are involved in human affairs and can be communicated with, petitioned, and befriended. They have become allies in magick to practitioners of many different traditions. Each archangel has dominion and responsibility over a particular area of creation, at least so much as humans understand it (chart 7). They take on very archetypal roles that are akin to both the classifications of pagan gods and modern psychological constructs. They are not, however, pagan gods in our understanding. Like humans, deities have a threefold nature, with their own passions, desires, agendas, faults, and blessings. One need only look at any book of mythology to see how "human" the gods can be. The gods display a full intersection of will, love, and wisdom, whereas the angels really embody only divine will. The angels can be thought of as the higher selves of the gods, but not the gods themselves. They are most prevalent in traditions that have a monotheistic worldview and deny or demonize the other spirit races, leaving only the angelic race accessible and available.

I tend to favor the Qabalistic system based on Jewish teachings, with each archangel associated with a sphere on the Tree of Life and named as the ruler of an order of angelic beings (chart 8). While the metaphor of a corporation with managers and works can help us understand the nature of angels, the metaphor of an organism, rather than an organization, can truly help us understand the intimate nature between the archangels and their orders. I've had one teacher describe the entire order as being the archangelic entity, while the individual angels of the order are like the cells within the body of that being. The archangel's body is vast, stretching across the cosmos. The angelic order move with one purpose, with one mind, but any one "cell" can represent the whole to a human.

Angelic Contact

Relax your body. Relax your mind. Open your heart. Feel the divine spark within. Engage the entire self for this working and prepare yourself for spiritual communion with the angelic realm. Invoke the straight line and call to the archangels and angels.

By the straight line,
I invoke the first ray.
I invoke the red ray.
I invoke the unbending ray of cold red archangelic flame.
I invoke the ray of will and power.

By the power of divine will,
I seek to know, feel, and enact divine will.
I seek contact with the angelic races.
Please make your presence known to me now.
So mote it be.

Envision the red light descending from the heavens in a pillar of cold flame. Find yourself surrounded by the red flame, a sparkling red metallic fire. Using your will, draw your awareness up this pillar of red fire and into the heavens. Find yourself entering a realm of soft, subtle starlight. Everything is white, milky brightness. Lights are twinkling, pleasantly, but there is no trace of shadow in this realm.

Within and around the light of the starry heavens, you feel the presence of the angelic races. There are more variations and individuality than you might have expected. Though an extension of divine will, each angel has its own essence and personality, working as part of the collective whole, just as we humans must do if we are to enter the next aeon. Each of us must embrace the paradox of retaining our uniqueness while being part of the greater whole by fulfilling our unique divine will.

An angelic figure steps forward to be your guide, making its individual presence known more clearly in this realm of light. The guide to the angelic realm wants to share with you the blessing of this world, and introduce you to the ministering angels of the seven sacred planets.

The light shifts to varying pulses of purple, silver, and yellow-white. Before you appear Archangel Gabriel and the angels of Luna. They communicate in words, images, and pulses of light. Take in any messages or secrets the angels of Luna have for you. They teach you about the will found in emotions and things that are concealed.

The Moon angels step back from your consciousness, and the light turns to orange and multicolored patterns of stripes and bands. Before you appear the Archangel Raphael and the angels of Mercury. They, too, wish to communicate with you. Be open to receiving any knowledge and information from the angels of Mercury.

The Mercurial angels step back from your awareness, and the light now turns to an emerald green flecked with pink. Before you appear the Archangel Haniel and the angels of Venus. They speak to you about the will found in passion and desire. One must want to enact divine will. Be open to receiving the passion from the angels of Venus.

The Venusian angels step back from your consciousness, and the light turns to a golden yellow, like the light of the Sun. Before you appear Archangel Michael and the angels of Sol. The Solar angels commune with you about necessary sacrifice and the harmony required to fulfill your divine will. Be open to receiving the messages of the angels of the Sun.

The Solar angels step back from your consciousness, and the light turns a ruby red. Before you appear Archangel Chamuel and the angels of Mars. Rather than offer you wisdom and advice, they test you. They ask you questions about the nature of your will and purpose. Be open to the testing of the angels of Mars.

The Martian angels step back from your awareness, and the light now turns a sky blue. Before you appear Archangel Tzadkiel and the angels of Jupiter. They want you to ask any question you have, and they will answer it truthfully. If you have a question for the angels, then ask.

The Jupiterian angels withdraw from your consciousness, and the light grows dim and dark, almost black like the night sky. The stars still twinkle along the inky blackness, yet the Archangel Tzafkiel and the angels of Saturn appear before you. They seek to show you the mysteries of understanding the divine will, beyond words and images. Be open to their mysteries.

The Saturnine angels draw back from your awareness, and the light returns to the soft starlight of when you began. An angelic ally for your personal journey steps forward, perhaps one you have already met or perhaps a new one. Take this time to commune with the angel.

When the experience is complete, feel your awareness slowly descend back down the pillar of metallic red fire. Move from the heavens to the Earth, and ground yourself as necessary.

Angelic mythology tells us that the angels were the first race created, for the will to create must come first, as the impetus to form and divide. The other races of creatures, particularly the fey and humans, have a relationship with the angelic races but remain separate from them. The study of one stream of life leads to greater understanding of all streams of life, and their reciprocal nature.

The Faery Races

In Christian mythology, the faery races have an intimate link with their kin from the realm of angels. In such stories, the faeries stemmed from those angels who developed some semblance of free will. According to various fallen angel stories, these angels became proud and disagreed with the Creator. They started a war of the heavens and lost, and were cast out. Other myths say they were asked to volunteer to enter the world—not just oversee it—and thereby mediate the Creator's love directly. In either case, the angels descended into matter, time, and space and became intimately tied to nature and the world.

In pagan myths there was no real "fall," but simply a change of cycles and seasons. The fey are an elder race that once was the dominant race of the world, but while they maintained their connections to the surface, they slowly withdrew to the Underworld to allow humans the space and time to grow. The fey oversaw the development of the planet and made the first magicks, but their nature, while in the world, was intangible and ephemeral. Though more realized than the angels in the material world, their nature was not quite flesh, blood, bark, or sap. They remained guardians of nature and are associated particularly with the woods and the land.

Today when you say the word faery, most people think of a tiny Tinkerbell-like figure of a small humanoid with butterfly or dragonfly wings flitting about. While some myths do speak of "little people," the oldest myths paint these beings as wise and powerful, sometimes larger than humans or even gigantic. The term faery goes back to the word *fata*, meaning "fate," and while we often think of faeries exclusively as nature spirits, the etymology of their name points to a far wider range of powers involving the nature of the Fates. Old myths relate them to the burial mounds of Europe and associate them with the world of the dead as much as the world of nature, for in those times the realms of the dead and of nature were thought of as more similar. Bodies were interred in the Earth, and Earth-reverent cultures looked to the realm below the Earth as the place of the dead, not a place of punishment.

Relationship with these spirits who dwell below has been considered an integral part of ages past. While faerylike lore can be explored worldwide, it is most prevalent in the Celtic and Germanic traditions, and came to the modern Witchcraft traditions from those cultures. A variety of beings are described, though their races and varieties are much like life, wild and chaotic. Faeries don't have the clearly defined structure of the angelic orders and choirs. Their differences are both cultural and regional, for our perception of beings tied to the land changes as the land itself changes. That is one of the reasons that immigrants to the United

States often would seek out areas that reminded them of home topographically, so similar bonds with the land could be forged.

Faeries were divided among the high and the low, similar to the archangels and angels in outer appearance. Humans describe the realm of the fey like a medieval court. The high fey are seen as royalty, kings and queens of their lands. The lower fey are described as members of the court. The lower fey are not trivial or unnecessary, as they support the rule of the high fey. They are part of an overall communal intelligence, like a colony of ants serving their queen for their overall good. Faeries are ruled by queen and king figures. Norse traditions call the land of the bright elves Alfheim, and that has come into British Witchcraft traditions as Elfame, or Elphame, land of the elves, where *elf* and *faery* are used synonymously. The Queen of Elphame is the Faery Queen, popularized in the folk tales of *Thomas the Rhymer* and *The Ballad of Tam Lin.*

While Irish myths describe the high fey as the Sidhe, pronounced "She," the Scottish myths call them the Sith, and describe a system of royal courts, the Seelie Court (good and kind faeries) and the Unseelie Court (evil and harmful faeries), arranged in a style similar to European royal courts. I'm not sure if the words good and evil are wholly appropriate when discussing faeries. Unlike the angels, the faery races are capable of making decisions. They mediate divine love, the love from nature, and not sentimental human love. Divine love can be both kind and cruel, and is not personal in its purest form. Yet many of us perceive ourselves as having personal relationships with the faeries.

More modern faery lore emphasizes the tiny, winged image popularized in the Victorian era, ultimately a beautiful, otherworldly female figure that is untouchable in any sexual way due to her size. There is the allure, yet the sense that such contact is wrong and literally off-limits, while previous faery lore often has the Faery Queen taking a lover to teach him the ways of Faerie and bless him with magickal gifts. Other theories state that the image of the faery has shrunk due to the amount of awareness we pay to their realm. As we perceive them less and less, they become smaller in stature to our senses. While they remain eternal, bright, and shining people of the dawn, our perception of them has shifted from a wise elder race linked with the ancestors, well respected and often feared, to playful, childlike, and often inconsequential nature spirits flitting about for our entertainment, sometimes making mischief by hiding our keys and other household items. Another branch of modern teachings equates the fair folk with the Hindu term deva, and usually presents them as vast intelligences with little of the personality and power of the older myths.

While these seem like wildly divergent ideas, I know practitioners who have had experiences with all three of these faery images. I've personally had contact and experience with all three, and I've sought a worldview of the faery folk that is true to my Witchcraft heritage yet does not invalidate these other genuine experiences people are having today. The nature of faeries seems to change depending on who is observing them. If you expect tiny, winged creatures, then you seem to get them. If you know the old myths, and expect the bright and shining people under the hills, then you experience a grander type of faery. This phenomenon echoes our quantum physics teaching, where the observer changes the outcome. Could all of these images be "right?" I asked my own faery contact to explain the differences in experiences and perceptions, and I was given a three-soul model for the faery races.

My own ally explained the turning of the mythical ages as the descent of some of the faery races deeper and deeper into the Earth and Underworld, further from the realm of the angels. While each race is always connected to nature and the green world, the consciousness of the faery race divided, with each anchoring itself in one of the three realms. They divided into the devas, nature spirits, and archfey for the Upper World, Middle World, and Lower World, respectively. The faery race on each plane of reality has an almost communal hive consciousness, differing from our distinct sense of individuality. They exist in a horizontal consciousness, across each plane of existence. Those in the deeper levels often are bound by territory. They are linked to a specific place, and barriers such as water or mountains can inhibit their group consciousness, so they have developed into specific clans. The faeries of Ireland are slightly different from those of England and Wales, and are even more different from those in the Americas, Africa, or Asia. Much as humans have developed racial types in accord with their environment, so have these deep fey.

Just like the three souls of humans, the three souls of nature, of this second ray, are not always clearly connected. They work best in community, with the three types of fey working together to manifest nature in a balanced and harmonious way. They work well with the races of flesh and blood, with animals and people. When we consume plant matter as food, or use natural materials in both our daily lives and our magick, we help forge deeper links vertically between the three worlds, as we exist in all three worlds with our three souls as well, across reality, forging links between the second and third rays. We can enhance these connections to each other simply through the reciprocal nature of breath, as we consciously breathe in their exhale of oxygen and they breathe in our exhale of carbon dioxide.

My faery ally then described the three general types of faery, relating to the three souls of nature.

Archfey

The archfey are the Sidhe, the Sith, the queens and kings of the faeries. The Sidhe is the Irish term for the Good People who live under the hill. This is the pagan association with the elder races who guided the Earth. They have descended and now fulfill a guardian role to nature, as the power within the land, unseen by most. They are described as the Lords and Ladies of Faerie, residing in their courts, and they come trouping out as if marching along special faery tracks. There are many other "races" of fey within their collective courts, also appearing as warriors, knights, jesters, and bards. They are the evolved spirits of the second ray. They are the spiritual masters and leaders of the fey. The archfey come in peace to those humans who honor the land and the old ways, and are constantly looking for allies on this side of the veil to aid them in their work to protect and preserve nature. They can act as allies, teacher, healers, and even companion friends. They also rise up in anger when nature has been desecrated or is in danger.

Nature Spirits

Nature spirits are those fey bonded with the Middle World. They are the consciousness of specific aspects of nature, such as plants, flowers, trees, and rocks. Each of the nature spirits is bonded with a specific part of nature, just as our Middle World consciousness, our sense of self, is bonded with our own body. But these nature spirits can extend their awareness, giving us the perception of smaller, winged creatures flitting about and buzzing around yet remaining in a generalized location where they "live." These individual spirits bond in larger groups, nature's "oversouls," creating the overall consciousness of a forest, a jungle, a field, or even a park.

Devas

The term devas, meaning "bright and shining," originally referred to the "little gods" of Hinduism, where everything in the cosmos has its own god. Every blade of grass and every grain of sand has its own deva. Today the term has come to mean the higher self, the god soul of nature. The domain of the devas is the Upper World, perhaps beneath angelic consciousness but the closest to angelic consciousness out of the three types of faery. In fact, some people do not use the word deva at all, but simply say nature angel. Each blade of grass may have its own deva, yet metaphysicians in the healing arts tend to focus on the overlighting deva of grass. Much as the archangels are the ruling consciousness of an order of angels, the overlighting deva is the ruling consciousness of a body of smaller devas, usually gathered together by species. All roses have an overlighting deva of roses, their collective higher self that holds the spiritual patterns of their species as well as all their medicinal and magickal information. The overlighting deva holds the archetype and information of the species. The overlighting deva, often simply and somewhat confusingly called just the deva, is a global consciousness of the Upper World. It is not the spirit of a specific rose bush. That specific spirit of an individual plant would be a nature spirit.

While at first this model of faery might seem overly complex, it neatly encapsulates a worldview where all these different perspectives on faeries can be understood and validated. Perception is the key. When looking at the faery races, the question you must ask is, are you looking at the Upper, Middle, or Lower World aspect? Traditions, or even simply personal biases that favor one of the worlds over another, will present a particular reality that is quite real but not necessarily a complete truth. It's like the old legend of the three blind men who visit an elephant, trying to understand such a strange creature they cannot see. One man touches the tail and describes the elephant as a poorly made fan. One touches the legs and describes them as two big trees with no branches. Another touches the trunk and describes it as a snake. Each is technically correct in describing a portion, but none of them understand the animal itself.

To better understand the relationships between the three selves, we can compare them to a modern construction project. The overlighting deva is like the architect, with the plans and designs. The individual deva is like the foreman on a particular job, overseeing operations and guiding the process. The nature spirits are like construction workers who build a specific building and then take up residence there, adding and breaking down parts as necessary. The Sidhe are like guardians, security, often unseen in day-to-day operations but present when needed. They make their base of operations in the basement and come up as required. They stay out of sight for the most part, watching and waiting. They also have their own lives, their own secret society, in this "basement."

The main purpose of the fey is the maintenance and development of the natural world. Their world can be enhanced by interaction with creatures of flesh and blood, leading to faery magick and even stronger spiritual alliances. Some say Witches of a particular flavor have faery "blood," and at one point, when the veil between the faeries and humans was not so thick, there was intermingling between the races. Descendants of human-faery matings, those with "the blood," are apt to have "the sight" of psychic ability and are more likely to practice magick and healing. Similar myths involving Witch blood tell of fallen angels mating with humans instead of faeries. Fallens angels are another perspective on the origin of the fey.

While the faeries can be petitioned for things, their tales emphasize the two-way nature of our relationship with them. It appears that making offerings to appease the fickle nature of the fey is the best way not only to ensure good crops or healthy animals and family members but also simply to maintain the status quo. When the faeries are not appeased, this leads to tales of their mischievous and even malevolent nature, sometimes wielding the forces of nature to the fullest extent. Many illnesses in the Anglo-Saxon traditions are attributed to "elfshot," an attack from the elves when they have been disturbed or dishonored. Similar teachings are found among the Celts. While these tales might sound crazy to modern people, ancient people knew the relationship between the land, the people, their livestock, and their food. In Tibetan medicine, there are rituals to appease the *nagas*, the serpent-like Earth spirits. If you disturb them, they can bring you illness, and if you appease them, they remove it, and can bring good health and good fortune. The offerings of both the fey and the naga are often white, symbolizing their "otherworldliness." Here, we have such a similar idea on the other side of the world of white offerings for the land spirits. As with the cycles of nature, the fey can bring bounty and blight, so offerings are made to keep the peace between humans who reside on the land and the faeries who reside in the land.

Faery Contact

Relax your body. Relax your mind. Open your heart. Feel the divine spark within. Engage the entire self for this working and prepare yourself for spiritual communion with the nature realm. Invoke the bent line and call to the faeries, devas, and nature spirits.

By the bent line,
I invoke the second ray.
I invoke the blue ray.
I invoke the spiraling ray of electric blue faery flame.
I invoke the ray of love and trust.
By the power of divine love,
I seek to know, feel, and enact Perfect Love and Perfect Trust.
I seek contact with the faery races.
Please make your presence known to me now.
So mote it be.

Feel the blue light rise out of the ground, spiraling around you like a corkscrew. Feel the blue flame dance around you, as if alive and filled with the life force of nature. Feel it surround your entire being, drawing you into a world of blue fire.

Gaze out into the world around you, as if you are looking through faint blue glass or blue crystal. Attracted to the light are the nature spirits of the world around you, the spirits of the lands and plants, the spirits of the stones and trees, the spirit of the very home or building where you are. The nature spirits have come to commune with you. Surrounded in this blue light of the second ray, they might be as curious about you as you are of them. They can easily pass in and out of the blue light, and when they do, you can better understand their thoughts, feelings, and intentions.

The nature spirits of the world between bring your awareness to the sky above. You notice the similarity between the blueness of the second ray and the color of the sky, and how some traditions believe that life force, prana itself, is blue. There is a presence above, a vast intelligence connected to the nature spirits around you. You sense the presence of the deva of this place, of these spirits. The deva appears to be operating on a similar but higher frequency of life. It is as if its communication with you is on a higher spiritual octave than that of the nature spirits, more ethereal and intellectual, more detached than the more visceral and childlike qualities of the nature spirits between.

Commune with the deva on the nature and purpose of this place, its history and its state of health. Commune with the deva on your purpose here with the land, with these nature spirits. The deva contains all the information, all from a "higher" perspective in the blue of the sky, seeing the big picture much like our own higher selves.

Feel yourself slowly sinking in the blue light, following the spiraling trail from which the light ascended. Feel yourself descending toward the source of this Underworld light, down into the kingdom of Faerie. The spiraling path leads you to the courts of Faerie, the country of Elphame, where the Queen and King reside as High Priestess and High Priest of this Underworld land. They mediate the flow of the blue faerie fire through the worlds, and their power protects nature. They are primal ones, members of the elder race that came before us. Many of us feel kinship with the fey, and find powerful teachers, allies, and healers among their kind. If you are welcomed into the Fey Court, take this time, with all courtesy and respect, to introduce yourself to the faery beings you encounter. You might find familiar faces, longtime friends, or childhood guides, or forge relationships that will last well into the future with those you encounter today.

When the experience is complete, feel your awareness slowly rise back up the spiral of blue fire. Move from the depths to the realm between, and ground yourself as necessary.

The only faerylike races not described in our three-soul model are those of the elementals. The consciousness of the four classical elements of fire, air, water, and earth often are described in terms of faery mythology, and do seem to have a kinship with our faery lore. Fire elementals are described as fiery salamanders, drakes, or fire faeries. Air elementals are called sylphs, matching the classic Victorian image of the faery. Water elementals are undines, the mermen and mermaids of myth. Earth elementals are described as dwarves, gnomes, or even goblins.

According to classical magickal teachings, the elementals are not fully evolved spirits with many aspects, but are a single-minded consciousness focused on one particular elemental drive and purpose. They aid us in our magick, for they learn much about mastering their elemental drive through contact with human magicians, Witches, and shamans. According to my faery contact, these beings of single-minded elemental consciousness have the opportunity to evolve, to learn to master multiple elements, and upon doing so, they can enter the realm of nature spirits. This shows that there are many forms of evolution in the streams of life.

The Human Races

The human races are both the easiest and the hardest for us to understand. Human races refer not only to the various skin colors, language sets, and ethnicities of the world today, often organized by Theosophists in the colors of red, yellow, white, black, and brown, but also to the races of humans in mythical civilizations predating our known history, including the tales of Atlantis, Lemuria, and Hybornea. In any of our mythologies, it appears that the human race, in all its forms, is the youngest of the three races, with our elders being the faeries and angels.

Unlike the angels, we humans are not naturally attuned to divine will. Much of our spiritual development and personal struggle can be a process of finding our own will, our own drive that is representative of the element of fire, and then refining that personal will from terrestrial fire into stellar fire, to align with the first ray and enact our divine will, the will that occurs when the three selves are in alignment and the flow of awen is moving through us.

Unlike the faeries, we are not naturally attuned to love, or even nature. For a variety of reasons, we feel and appear separate from nature, though our origin is much like that of any other animal. The leap from a hunter-gatherer tribal society to agrarian farmers has separated us from our animal kin. The use of abstract language, writing, and sophisticated tools, as well as building permanent structures, has further separated us. We mythologize this experience as the fall from the Garden, leaving paradise, or the collapse and sinking of a motherland civilization. All of these myths are true on some level. What we have gained on one level we have lost on another. But this is part of our work, as the embodiment of the crooked line, the third ray. We must separate in order to be connected again. Like the process of alchemy, where chemicals and plants are subjected to stressful forces, dissolved, separated, and recombined, we, too, undergo this process, personally and as a race, as part of our service to the streams of evolution and the Creator, the Goddess, God, and Great Spirit.

Of the three races, humans are the one with the greatest weaknesses and the greatest potential. We don't have any natural qualities to draw from, be it divine will or nature's love. We have the potential for wisdom, which comes through knowledge and experience. To truly embody that wisdom, we must connect the other two powers, will and love. Like a serpent moving back and forth, choosing will then love, will then love, we weave connections between the races of the heavens and the races of the Underworld. By connecting the two powers and connecting the worlds above and below, the bonds of creation are strengthened. All the parts can then know each other, and thereby better know themselves. Through our work, creation develops. Each of the races has a part to play, and ours is simply the connecting role. Having free will, we have the capacity for divine will while simultaneously having the capacity to choose love. It's a hefty responsibility, but we're the only ones to do it.

The animal world has evolved to a point where we have the option of separating, so in our temporary isolation we can grow from a new perspective, and return with this wisdom. Those who are not in isolation, our animal kin, serve as our first teachers, our totem animals and fetch beasts, for they hold the keys to return. They have never left. They remind us of the wisdom and lessons we forgot in our separation, and we bring to them new experiences not dreamt of in the animal kingdom. In essence, all creation is an extension of the divine, to grow rich from experience, to develop true wisdom from that experience, and a return to the source to thereby enrich the whole.

There are many individuals who have already simultaneously chosen will, love, and wisdom, and our prophecies of a new Golden Age envision a time when all humans will do this and return from isolation. These wise masters from every age and every tradition have many names. They now guide those who walk the path they have walked. They are known as the Selfless Saints, the Justified Ones, the Order of Blessed Souls, or the bodhisattvas. In pagan times, these enlightened individuals were referred to as the demigods. The best example is Hercules, who had both human and divine parents and underwent a series of trials, twelve labors, that eventually led to his ascent to Olympus, the home of the gods. While his story can be one of a Greek folk hero elevated to divine status, it is also a secret teaching of enlightenment, through twelve key teachings modeled after the signs of the zodiac. To the Norse, these wise masters are the Einherjar, those elevated for their heroism, chosen by the Valkyries for the paradise hall among the gods to await the last days when Ragnarok will come. To the Theosophist, they are the Great White Brotherhood, the Ladies and Lords of Shamballa, the ascended masters. To the ceremonial magician, they are the Secret Chiefs, the Inner Plane Adepts, the Withdrawn Order, and the Inner Convocation. To the tribal people, they are the deified ancestors, the Grandmothers and Grandfathers of Long Ago. And to the Witch, they are the Mighty Dead, priests and priestesses who died with might and power, who guide the tradition. They are the Hidden Company who gather at the edge of our circles. They are the Timeless Tradition of our Nameless Art.

The Hidden Company are those who have found the path to consciously choose to enact their divine will in every moment, while simultaneously choosing to embody divine love found in nature in every moment. Through their spiritual practice and craft, through the application of knowledge and experience, the Serpent of Wisdom has fully grown within them. They have expanded their consciousness and united their three selves on a permanent basis, unshaken by the experiences of life, and joined this illustrious order.

Our Mighty Dead continue to guide us. As they have carved a path to this level of union and enlightenment, they maintain links between our race and tradition and those of the angels and fey. They have been responsible for the modern resurgence and regeneration of the Craft. They have done so not only to change the path that humanity is on but also to find, from the growing crowd of Witches and occultists, those who are ready to make the leap, in small and large ways, to unite love and will to find wisdom and build bridges between humanity, angel, and fey. They guide us covertly and overtly, in whispers, dreams, and intuition and through vision and ritual. They are our teachers and healers and guides on the path, and who better to show us the way than those who have already successfully walked it, and stepped off the wheel of rebirth whole, to stand in the place between timeless and nameless, waiting for us.

Contact with the Hidden Company grants us this greater source of wisdom, teaching, power, and love, for their information supersedes that of all earthly agencies. In fact, the rituals and traditions that survive in our Craft ultimately are used to guide us to these Mighty Ones, and the gods that stand with them. Once we've established contact with them, we have our source of deeper wisdom readily available.

Contact with the Hidden Company

Relax your body. Relax your mind. Open your heart. Feel the divine spark within. Engage the entire self for this working and prepare yourself for spiritual communion with the realm of the Mighty Dead. Invoke the crooked line and call to the Hidden Company.

By the crooked line,
I invoke the third ray.
I invoke the yellow ray.
I invoke the crooked ray of serpentine gold Witch fire.
I invoke the ray of wisdom and cunning.
By the power of divine wisdom,
I seek to know, feel, and enact divine wisdom and cunning.
I seek contact with the Mighty Dead, the Hidden Company of Witches,
The Timeless Order of the Nameless Art.
Please make your presence known to me now.
So mote it be.

Feel a lightning bolt simultaneously descend from the heavens and rise from the depths, a bolt of golden white light flashing with inspiration and insight for one brief moment, illuminating all the worlds, followed by utter darkness. You are surrounded by the darkness of the void, the darkness of the outer spaces that reach all around us in the Great Between.

Then, on the edge of your vision, you see golden yellow flames, like stars coming into view. They illuminate the darkness and appear to be moving closer to you, forming a ring around you. Look down at your chest, and you will find a similar light, a tiny star within glowing brightly, though not as brightly as those surrounding you.

The stars form a perfect ring around you, and are glowing in the heart of the spirit forms of the Mighty Dead, the Witches of the Hidden Company. Before you and behind you, to the left and right, are the integrated souls of the Witch masters, the ancestors of our Timeless Tradition, the masters of our Nameless Art. They have united power, love, and wisdom. They have unlocked the mysteries of the three rays. They have made allies above, below, and between. They are you in potential. You are waiting to become one of them.

One or more of these figures might step forward from the circle and commune with you. One might be your mentor, your teacher in our tradition, or several may act as advisors, aiding you in your own particular mission in this life, in this world, for our order. You might feel as if you are being passed from one master to the next, not in a circle but across the circle, forming a crooked zigzagging of lines like a net or web. Commune with the Mighty Ones.

When the experience is complete, watch the starry hearts of the Hidden Company step back, further and further with each second. They no longer gather at the edge of your circle but extend ever outward into the universe, fading from your vision but ever present in your awareness. One day you, too, could be like them. Feel the lightning bolt rise again from the depths while descending from the heavens, filling your world with a flash of light and wisdom. Then the darkness is dispelled and you are surrounded by the world you know. Bring your awareness completely back from the power of the crooked line. Ground and balance yourself as needed.

The nature of the Hidden Company can be difficult to understand. We each have our own concept of what "enlightenment" is, yet trying to describe enlightenment without having it is much like trying to describe sex if you've never had it. It is a mystery that can never quite be put into words, but those who experience it find a kinship and connection that goes beyond words. The grand assembly of Mighty Dead, from a Theosophical view, are called the ascended masters. They transcend tradition, culture, ethnicity, and time period. Much of the early literature tends to favor masters with an Eastern expression, leading to a belief in the West that the stereotype of Eastern enlightenment was the standard for all. We still have a vision of an "enlightened" person as being this totally peaceful, passive, detached individual, yet not all cultures subscribe to that aesthetic. Pagan cultures value honor, skill, cunning, and courage as much as any other trait. In truth, such masters might seem dominated by one of the three rays, and more often dominate by either the powers of love and mercy or of power and severity, but enlightenment comes through the balance and synthesis of the three. I don't think I can truly describe enlightenment other than the union of love, will, and wisdom in its most impersonal form. The vision of the three rays gives us a philosophy and a mode of operation, but until we understand what it means to us and then fully embody it, we will not experience this mystery.

Thankfully, the concept of enlightenment subsequently has been developed, revealing that the masters come from all traditions of wisdom, and in truth are somewhat beyond gender, appearance, and even individual consciousness. At their level of consciousness, they realize they are individual expressions of one primal power. They choose the appearance of previous incarnations most conducive to communing with us, and although each facet of this group consciousness might have a specific focus, they operate as a collective. Masters who ascend through the Witchcraft traditions will feel a special kinship with Witches. Masters of the Christian traditions will more likely guide Christians. Messages have come through from the tribal masters, and hopefully soon there will be more recognition of the masters from pagan, heathen, and Witchcraft traditions in the more mainstream metaphysical movement.

The three races work together and also have their own evolutionary paths. According to occultists, the mineral realm holds an entranced consciousness, one that is not aware of time and space as we know it. Their guiding race, the angels, hold the power of stasis in their consciousness. They are unwavering in their awareness. The plant realm holds a sleeping consciousness in relationship to humans. Their faery guardians hold the power of repetition found in the cycles of nature. And the creatures of flesh and blood hold a dreaming consciousness and, in humanity, at least from our perspective, a waking consciousness. Animals and particularly humans hold the power to change, breaking from stasis and enacting change.

The Gods

We could see the Hidden Company as godlike, though to some Witches that thought would be blasphemous. Among those of us truly in the Nameless Art, we know there is power in blasphemy, in treading where others fear to go and undoing the expectations of self and other. Such work releases a tremendous amount of energy bound up in fear and dogma that could be put to better use for our own enlightenment and the evolution of the world. So in walking that path, it is easy to see the Mighty Dead as godlike.

Where are the gods on our three ray scheme of evolution? What evolutionary path do they follow, or is the evolution of a god a contradictory concept? I believe the gods are creatures of all three rays. They embody will, love and wisdom in various proportions. The three rays are like the three selves of the Creator, and any entity that embodies all three is considered godlike. When we look at the pagan myths, particularly those of Northern Europe, it can be quite difficult to tell who is mortal and who is a god. The status of their mortality seems to ebb and flow, and change with the story. Some get elevated to the status of godhood and leader of the gods, such as in the story of Lugh knocking on the door of Tara. Others, such as Macha, assume human roles and then, if insulted or injured, return to a defied state and leave the world of mortals. Conceivably some ancestral spirits evolve due to the veneration of their people, forming the nucleus of a god. Many believe figures such as the Norse Odin were once tribal leaders whose human origins dissolved in the mists of time. With enough veneration, Odin's story changed to that of a superhuman who, along with his brothers, is credited with creating the nine worlds from the remains of an ice giant. His human roots are left behind entirely. We already can see very human-acting mythical figures such as King Arthur and Merlin taking on a demigod status. If the trend continues, who's to say they won't eventually be considered gods of an Arthurian pantheon separate from human history and evolution?

I believe the gods are those who embody all three aspects of will, love, and wisdom. Some are issued forth with all three, while others attain this status over time. They could come from the ranks of humanity, from the ascended ones, but over time evolve into the status of gods. They could come from any race, for if one from the realm of the faeries or angels somehow learns to embody the other two qualities, then what are they but a god? The fallen angels of the Grigori, the Watchers, who father the giant Nephilim when the "Sons of God" mate with the "Daughters of Man," appear to be gods in their power and scope. A few Witchcraft traditions honor them as both gods and ancestors. The Tuatha de Danaan, the race of gods in ancient Ireland, are considered to be faeries by some, but are obviously also gods. Perhaps their origin was with the faery races, and that is where they returned upon the coming of humanity. The origins of the gods are many, birthed, evolved, abstract, and personal, and are one of the mysteries, but a mystery worth pursuing as you unite love, power, and wisdom.

Those Who Dwell Outside

The only races that remain untouched by the three rays are those that come from the "outside." Though theologically most Witches believe that everything is divine, that everything seen and unseen is a manifestation of the Great Spirit, there are other manifestations beyond and outside of ours. Imagine many universes, each stemming from a central source. Like a snowflake, each axis extending outward is like its own universe, joined with the others in the center (figure 9). We have a creation of three rays, manifesting in three worlds, giving a ninefold plot of reality. All the entities native to our reality come from that axis. The other five axes of our snowflake may or may not have the same structure. Entities that cross over from those universes are those that come from the "outside" and feel alien to our consciousness. Their tales are encoded in the fallen angel, ancient astronaut, and elder god mythoi, and, for the purpose of this work, play no role in our evolution of the three rays.

FIGURE 9: UNIVERSAL SNOWFLAKE

CHAPTER SIX:
THREE WAYS OF MAGICK

For there are three great events in the life of man—love, death and
resurrection in the new body—and magic controls them all. To fulfill
love you must return again at the same time and place as the loved
ones, and you must remember and love her or him again. But to be
reborn you must die and be ready for a new body; to die you must
be born; without love you may not be born, and this is all the magic.
—"The Descent of the Goddess," Gardnerian Book of Shadows

Ours is a craft, and the power of a craft comes not from the thinking and conjecture, but from putting our art into application. Witchcraft is what you do, not necessarily what you think or believe. Magick is at the heart of our Craft, though many seeking out a form of spirituality often reject the art of magick as something impure and unspiritual. Nothing could be further from the truth for a Witch. For us, all things are sacred. All things are divine, from the bliss of universal consciousness to making sure we have food on our table, a roof over our head, and a fulfilling sexual partner. In fact, an old pagan philosophy is summed up in the blessing and closing "FFFF," which stands for Flags, Flax, Fodder, and Frigg, or simply Flagstones (Home), Flax (Clothing), Fodder (Food), and Frigg (Love/Sex).

We are called to be a practical, balanced people, wanting neither too little nor too much, but finding a harmony with the resources we need and satisfying our desires. Only when we have our basic needs and wants met can we truly put our energy into more lofty pursuits. Those who examine their basic needs and wants have a great advantage in opening the gates to the mysteries. All acts of magick are an opportunity for enlightenment. The simplest of spells can reveal great things to us.

I believe that when we do all our magick with the intention of it being "for the highest good" or "in accordance with divine will," the magick becomes a teacher. By watching what works and what doesn't, we begin to discern the direction of our higher will, and examine the things we feel we want and need that don't appear to be in alignment with our higher will. If a spell doesn't work, then we first must determine if our spellcraft was faulty. Was something in the process, in the technique of magick, out of alignment? Magick is a science, with a reasonable set of criteria. When the criteria are followed properly, the process yields results. If we can find no fault in our Craft, and we continue on this path but still with no results, then we must question if the intention itself is contrary to our divine will, the pattern held by our higher self. If we are not in conscious relationship with this higher god self, our Watcher, then our magick provides an opportunity for it to speak to us, by telling us yes or no.

While there are many methods of dividing and categorizing magick, for our work here we naturally divide each of the three rays into sets of three (chart 9). Each ray has an inherent property and generates a different form of magick when manifested in the Upper, Lower, or Middle World. Each of these forms of magick leads to a different door to the mysteries, as each has a natural ally among the three streams of life. Such allies can act as teachers and tutors. Following the types of magick of one ray brings you a deep understanding of that ray. Working jointly with different types of magick is a slower process, yet yields a broader understanding of the mysteries and grants a thorough experience of our Craft.

Ray	Practical Magick Middle World	Discipline Lower World	Art and Science Upper World	Ally
First ray	Blessing/cursing	Mineral	Alchemy/smithing	Angel
Second ray	Prosperity	Plant	Medicine/gardening	Faery
Third ray	Romance/lust	Animal	Husbandry/ midwifery	Animal

CHART 9: MAGICK OF THE THREE RAYS

Magick can be divided into different levels of detail and complexity and according to its ultimate purpose. Magick of the Middle World is often folk magick and practical. It is useful for those seeking to solve their immediate problems and fill their immediate needs. Though any experienced practitioner is capable of effectively casting such magick, even those without this earned power can successfully work this magick. Much of it involves using formulas, traditions, and the inherent power of the objects and symbols in the Middle World to affect things in this realm. Though this type of magick is sacred, there is no great mystery involved in its working, and most who perform it experience no divine mystery. It can, however, lead to a deeper understanding of how magick works, and potentially open the door to the mysteries.

Magick of the Lower World is the more detailed crafts of correspondence. Practitioners work with a body of lore, and develop knowledge of and relationships with that lore, in the form of material vessels. Yet the wise practitioner has an animistic view of these vessels, communing with the spirit of each and establishing a relationship with them. The corresponding tools cease to be tools and instead become our allies and friends. They become our teachers. Listening to them unlocks the secrets of nature and gives us access to the profound power, love, and wisdom.

Magick of the Upper World is the greater disciplines, the holy arts and science that become a way of life if practiced properly. They have many interconnections, for one holy art leads to another, and all are encompassed by our holy art, science, and religion of the Craft. But each leads to a particularly deep insight into the nature of life from the perspective of its ray.

Magick of the Straight Line

The magick of the first ray is all magick involving the application of power. We define magick in classical terms from the work of Aleister Crowley as "the art and science of causing change in conformity with Will." So technically all magick requires will, but some forms of magick resonate more clearly with the first ray. The most desired and feared application of power in the Witch's toolbox falls under the first ray. It is the power to bless and to curse—two sides of the same coin, for both are an application of power directed at another. The only difference is if the power is held with benevolent intention, to bless, or with malevolent intention, to blast. Power is power; it is only the application, circumstance, and result that differentiate it. On the more practical side, the power to protect, to accept energy only consciously and not have it be forced upon you, is another practical application of the first ray. It is the use of power to block, deflect, avoid, and absorb. It is the power to remain unaffected by anyone's will but your own. This is the Middle World use of the first ray most often desired by Witches and non-Witches: the power of the shield.

Blessing

The term *bless* may derive from the practice of consecrating people by sprinkling blood, as the life force of the blood provides the life force for the consecration. Today, salt water, fresh water, sacred oil, or simply intention usually are used in place of blood. But the concept of life force and power found in blood and associated with blessing should not be forgotten. This is a simple blessing to be done for yourself or another, silently or out loud, with or without a consecration fluid.

Take a moment to center and align yourself. Feel the power of the three cauldrons within you. Feel the power of your life force, emotion, and inspiration be touched with the raw power of the first ray. Feel the first ray energy stoke your own power. Feel that power rise up and out your hands. Touch the recipient of the blessing with this intention:

> *Blessed be your body, protected from all harm.*
> *Blessed be your heart, open to the love, joy, and happiness.*
> *Blessed be your mind, clear in word and thought.*
> *Blessed be your life, may every deed bring you power, love, and wisdom.*
> *So mote it be.*

Feel the power pass with your intention, and let it work its magick. Ground yourself as needed.

Cursing

Some might consider it unethical to curse and to teach cursing in a text such as this. But because cursing is the flip side of blessing, it is imperative to know how curses work, and have the power to do them. What you direct a curse at is up to you and your own ethics. One can curse an illness to wither and leave good health, or curse a murderer to be caught by the police. One could argue that any type of destructive or waning Moon magick, including forms of healing and helping, technically could be considered a curse.

To perform a simple curse, prepare as you did for the blessing, though traditional sources say the best classical curses are done with the power of justice, anger, or vengeance in your heart. An able-bodied practitioner can do this work through will and power, and not necessarily through emotion. Emotion is just one way to fuel your energy. Though I might be emotional when doing healing work to remove someone's illness, I'm not angry at the illness, but I've helped the recipient stoke up their "I'm going to fight it" mindset. Many of the most successful recoveries involve having the patient envision thoroughly defeating, even destroying, their illness.

Center and align yourself. Feel the power of the three cauldrons within you and the power you gather with the first ray. Hold your intention and direct the power with your hands, directly or over a distance.

I curse you to wither and wane.
I curse you to diminish.
I blast and blight you until your power means nothing to me.
So mote it be.

Feel the power pass with your intention, and let it work its magick. Ground yourself as needed.

Protection Spell

Protection magick is used to prevent anyone from influencing you in a way you do not desire, whether the person does it with malice and harm or with meddling good intentions. Protection magick directs your energy outward and acts as a shield, blocking or grounding unwanted forces, like a trap detaining energies, or like an incinerator, destroying unwanted forces before they actually reach you.

While protection magick comes in a variety of charms, incantations, and visualizations, this version, like the previous blessings and curses, is based on your own power.

Center and align yourself. Feel the power of the three cauldrons within you and the power you gather with the first ray. Feel the presence of an energy field around you, as if your three cauldrons exist within the center of a larger cauldron that extends a bit farther than your arm in every direction. Hold your protection intention and direct the power out and around you in every direction, filling this larger cauldron and coating the outside edges. Your intention programs this energy on the edges. Say:

I hallow my protection shield,
Preventing all harm—positive, negative, or otherwise—from reaching me.
May it ground and transform all that does not serve my highest good,
While allowing in the blessings and magick I desire,
And reflecting back balanced love, power, and wisdom upon the source of the harm.
So mote it be.

The Lower World application of the first ray is working with mineral, metals, and crystals. While this might seem like the domain of the faery races, many legends tell of certain metals and materials being baneful to the fey, particularly iron and its derivative, steel. While the growing plants and trees appear to suit the nature of the bending ray, the solidness of metals and minerals suits the unyielding position of the straight ray. One of the reasons crystal magick and healing are so effective is that, for all practical purposes, the matrix of the mineral locks the divine purpose, the will, of the mineral into place. There is little that can change the true purpose, the divine will, of a mineral, at least not without great effort. The seven alchemical metals of lead, tin, iron, copper, quicksilver, silver, and gold are said to be the stars within the Earth, the reflections of light from Saturn, Jupiter, Mars, Venus, Mercury, Moon, and Sun held within the Underworld. They undergo their own evolutionary process when untouched by the light of the Moon or Sun, evolving up the ladder, from lead to gold, refining their own consciousness.

While this concept might seem absurd to the chemist, the alchemist would argue that metals behave in a manner consistent with the laws of chemistry only when exposed to the light of the world and the "rules" of the Middle World, as understood by practitioners of chemistry, biology, and physics. Within the dark womb of the Underworld, other rules apply. At first I was skeptical of this concept, though the philosophy now parallels the classic thought experiment known as Schrödinger's Cat. Basically this experiment involves a scenario of a sealed steel box with a vial of poison and a cat, and a device using radioactive decay to potentially signal a hammer device to shatter the poison vial and kill the cat. The observer cannot know if the device has been activated yet, so the cat is both alive and dead in a superposition of states according to quantum law. The act of opening the box and observing is what makes the result, the living or dead cat, exist. According to this work, there is no single outcome until the reality is observed. So if we are not able to observe the metals and minerals, then perhaps they are undergoing their own unknown evolutionary process. Even if not a literal fact, Schrödinger's Cat provides an excellent philosophical basis for work with minerals and metals specifically and magick in general.

Angels have not always been associated with minerals and stones, yet have you noticed, in this modern age, how many people who are drawn to angelic lore and teachings also are fascinated with the use of crystals for healing and personal development? There is a connection there, as each is a key to finding divine will. Those who feel called to the magick of the straight path seek it out through the allies of the angels, as well as the mineral spirits, those who act like a mirror to the angels while growing in the Underworld. Out of the three races, angels are potentially the most powerful but also the most disconnected, for they have a manifestation in the heavens and rule over the world but they have no true manifestation in the world of form. Those angels that do descend end up in the realm of Faerie and have a manifestation through the plant world. The heavenly angels are matched only by the metals and minerals in the Underworld. The only manifestation of the angelic power in a tangible form is through minerals, and the minerals only make their way into the Middle World when brought upward from the depths, usually by human effort. The crystals can mediate divine will (chart 10).

Crystal	Magickal Properties
Amber	Wealth, protection, absorbing and projecting energy
Amethyst	Prosperity, soberness, clarity, peace
Aquamarine	Attunement with the sea, psychic power, blessings
Aventurine	Wealth, health, good fortune
Bloodstone	Blood purifier, protector, warrior
Calcite	Reflection, understanding, overcoming fears
Carnelian	Energy, drive, focus, communication, health
Citrine	Energy, health, success, wealth, inspiration
Emerald	Love, clear sight, healing, prosperity, purpose
Fluorite	Protection, clear aura, boundaries
Garnet	Energy, grounding, power
Hematite	Protection, grounding
Jade	Healing, immortality, luck, prosperity
Jet	Protection, Underworld, ancestors
Peridot	Love, heart healing, wealth, happiness
Kyanite	Clearing the mind, focusing on goals, clarity of purpose
Lapis lazuli	Prosperity and abundance, beauty, sacredness
Malachite	Communion with nature, grounding, protection
Moldavite	Communion with the heavens, protection, psychic power
Moonstone	Psychic power, emotional healing, dreams
Moss agate	Boundaries, healing the skin, attunement with nature
Obsidian	Protection, divination, psychic power
Onyx	Grounding, mourning, karma, responsibilities, strength, blocking magick
Pyrite	Wealth, health, true purpose
Quartz	All magick, amplification of thoughts, psychic ability
Rose quartz	Self-love, healing, creativity, connection
Ruby	Energy, drive, willpower
Sapphire	Communication, clarity, purpose behind words
Selenite	Connection with spirit, past lives, spirit guidance
Tiger's eye	Protection, purpose, energy
Tourmaline	Grounding (black), healing (green), love (pink)
Turquoise	All-purpose, protection, eloquence, peace, healing

CHART 10: STONE CORRESPONDENCES

Crystal Charm

A very simple crystal charm can be made from a moonstone. Obtain a small piece of moonstone that will rest comfortably on your forehead when you are lying on your back. All stone charms should be cleansed first. To cleanse the stone easily and completely, you can run it under cold water for a few minutes, or pass it through the smoke of a purifying incense, such as a frankincense and myrrh combination, sage, or copal.

Lie down and place the cleansed stone upon your brow. Hold the cleansed stone there with your hand for a moment and, using the method of blessing described earlier in this chapter, bless the stone with power and intention, specifically with the intention of increasing psychic power, ability, and accuracy.

I hallow this stone for psychic power.
Grant me the blessings of vision, hearing, touching, tasting, smelling, and knowing,
Through the senses beyond.
Grant me accuracy in knowing what was, what is, and what will be,
For the highest good, harming none.
So mote it be.

Relax your hand for a bit, and just allow this new perception to come over you, as your brow interacts with the crystal. Do you feel any different? When ready, remove the crystal, and get up and and ground yourself as needed by releasing excess energy into the land, and becoming more present to your physical body. Stomping your left foot three times can help, and in more severe cases, eating will ground you. Notice the difference in your psychic ability when you carry the stone and when you don't.

The highest art of the magick of the straight line, beyond simple correspondence, is the art of alchemy. It is the Upper World magick of the first ray, to duplicate the process of the Deeper Earth within your laboratory and your consciousness, and to birth golden stars in your awareness. One of the reasons alchemy has been so easy to absorb and adapt to Christian mysticism in its European branches is that so much of its work is in accord with the Upper World, as it seeks to refine something "lower" into something that is "higher." Unknown to most who think of alchemy simply as a get-rich-quick scheme, European alchemists would spend much time in preparation praying in shrines that were part of the laboratory before undertaking their experiments, believing their state of consciousness to have just as much bearing on the operation as the operation itself and the materials involved. Angelic figures can be seen in the alchemical engravings. Even one of the most popular images of the alchemical process, found in the tarot card Temperance, has an angelic figure standing between land and water, mixing together fluids poured from two different vessels (figure 10). Future magicians and tarot artists have renamed this trump Art, or even directly Alchemy, and further enhanced the imagery.

Though alchemy might seem a far cry away from Witchcraft, similar mysteries based on the transformation of metals, if not the same philosophical history, can be found in smithcraft, an art intimately associated with Witchcraft. Blacksmiths were considered village magicians in much the same way the Cunning Woman or Cunning Man was, as all did something unknown to the average person, thereby doing magick. While the blacksmith and the alchemist seem worlds apart, the Temperance card also links them, for the art of tempering metals truly is an alchemical process.

FIGURE 10: TEMPERANCE CARD

Magick of the Bent Line

The magick of the second ray is also threefold. While the second ray is the ray of divine love, in the Middle World it manifests as the magick of prosperity. It rules over prosperity because of its associations with the power of nature, the power of green and growing things. Prosperity is not just money magick, and it certainly isn't abundance magick. It's not about getting and hoarding things; it's about thriving, and having all the resources you need and want to thrive. To prosper really means to grow. But in the process of natural prosperity, there is an exchange. There are cycles of life and death to prosperity. The Greek goddess Persephone, the loved and feared Queen of the Underworld, brings both death and life, for only with both death and life is there a harvest. Persephone's Roman name is Proserpine. Though the etymology of the name is related to "creeping forward" in terms of sprouting plants and possibly serpents, her name often is spelled, perhaps erroneously, Prosperine, reminding us of the word prosperity and our intuitive understanding of the connection between prosperity, life, and death.

You must make room for the things you want by getting rid of the things you don't need. What you give up and what you give out can feed the cycles of prosperity for others. In magick, and particularly in Witchcraft, we talk about the power of return. Energy ultimately returns to its source. On the lowest level of awareness, this principle operates as what people perceive as the reward and punishment of "karma." On the highest level, the principle of return operates in the structure of the Qabalah, the Tree of Life, when the divine emanates forth to create the ten worlds, and then that which it has issued forth seeks to return to the source, wiser and more experienced than before. That is why we all seek reunion with the divine, with our source. It is the impulse of return. When we aid people, and, in fact, when we aid any race of flesh or spirit, in their own flourishing and prosperity, the energy of prosperity returns to feed us.

Within prosperity workings, there is an opportunity to understand the true meaning of prosperity and to flourish through balanced exchange and harmony with those around us. While desperation of need or overwhelming desire can drive us to this magick in the first place, there is a powerful mystery to be awakened if we can keep our awareness focused on a larger purpose as we satisfy our wants and needs.

Prosperity Spell

When the Moon is waxing, mix equal parts of cinnamon, clove, and nutmeg. Bless them with the intention of prosperity using the blessing technique described earlier in this chapter. Burn them on charcoal, fumigating the entire home or business. Then mix equal parts of basil leaves, lemon peel, and rose petals blessed for prosperity. Add two tablespoons of the mix to two cups of boiling water and let steep for a half hour. Add that to water in a wash bucket, and anoint your door and window frames and wash your floors with it. Next, beneath a houseplant that grows well, bury three copper coins blessed for prosperity, along with a piece of paper on which you have written the names of any material objects you want or, if you require a specific amount of money, an amount. If you do not need a specific item or amount of money, then simply write the word "prosperity" on the paper. Ask the Green Gods that this come in a spirit that is for your highest good, harming none. Your prosperity will come to you.

The Underworld magick of the second ray is the art of plant magick. While herbs and roots are used in Middle World magick to form charms for protection, prosperity, and romance, their deeper magick comes in building a relationship with the green world. The nature spirits of the herbs, and their respective devas, open us to a much richer world of magick. Heartfelt working with the land and the plants through magick also can attract the attention of the archfey, who will teach you even more about the mysteries of nature.

On the surface, much of magickal herbal lore seems to be dedicated to money, love, lust, protection, success, cursing, and fertility. Most spells will fit in those categories, more or less. Plant magick certainly can be used for all of these things, but as you explore your relationships with the plants, you will realize that each one is a spirit, each one is a guide. Each one can act like a totem for you, and bring its blessings. Just as no two people are exactly alike, and each can show you something different, each species of plant is different and can teach you something different. Two protection herbs protect differently, and each has a lesson. Each love herb attracts love differently. The only question is, who will be your teacher?

Herbal magick opens the door to transforming consciousness, from entheogenic rituals that induce trance and facilitate spirit contact, to herbal formulas that make alterations in the energies of the human body, granting psychic abilities, magickal powers, and aligning your consciousness with the deepest powers of your soul (chart 11).

Plant	Magickal Properties
Angelica	Protection, healing, angelic contact
Basil	Prosperity, sexuality, attraction
Chamomile	Relaxation, peace, health, psychic vision, dream magick
Cinnamon	Prosperity, wealth, clarity, warmth
Comfrey	Regeneration, past-life recall, preventing the loss of objects, protection
Dandelion	Grounding, wealth, summoning spirits, wishes, healing anger
Datura	Spiritual journey, psychic power, Goddess energy, love, seduction, sex
Elecampane	Faery contact
Fennel	Eloquence, protection when traveling, weight loss
Foxglove	Faery contact, love magick, healing the heart
Frankincense	Purification, sacred space, protection, enlightenment, wealth, health
Garlic	Protection, purification, victory, cursing
Horsetail	Regeneration, clearing karma, protection
Lady's mantle	Communion with nature, Goddess energy, youth, feminine healing
Lavender	Peace, tranquility, clear thought, clear words, cleansing, healing, dreams
Lemon balm	Supports all magick, calmness, psychic powers, dreams
Licorice	Energizing, breaking addictions, power, sweetness
Myrrh	Cleansing, protection, purification, karma
Nettle	Protection, faery contact, letting go of harm
Parsley	Protection, Underworld communion, cleverness, cursing
Red clover	Good fortune, Goddess energy, prosperity
Rose	All magick, love, healing, mysteries, Goddess energy
Rue	Protection, blessings, love, money, health
Sage	Purification, rejuvenation, cleansing, health
Scullcap	Memory, clear thought, communication, peacefulness
Slippery elm	Healing the throat, stopping gossip
St. John's wort	Healing trauma, preventing nightmares, protection, health, spiritual guidance
Valerian	Sleep, dreams, ancestors
Yarrow	Protection, love, faery contact

CHART 11: PLANT CORRESPONDENCES

You can work with the wisdom of a particular plant by carrying that plant around with you as a talisman. Dried leaves, flowers, and stems can be carried in a charm pouch, or the essential oil can be carried in a decorative vial. My favorite method is to carry the root as a "fetish" or charm. The most famous of these charms is created with the mandrake plant, which is powerful and difficult to obtain. It's known as a "manakin" and is said to act like a Witch's familiar, protecting the home and doing her bidding, like a wooden homunculus.

Other plants with strong roots can be crafted into talismans. The root often is dried, then anointed with scented oils, and carried in a pouch to confer the blessings of the root upon you. Practitioners of Hoodoo use the root of High John the Conqueror. I myself have used the roots of angelica, Solomon's seal, comfrey, and datura quite successfully. Such charms require you to meditate with the plant spirit, ask its permission to be used in such a way, and then make an offering to the plant, perhaps coins, milk and honey, beer or wine. You should harvest the root secretly and dry it in the dark, checking in with it often and speaking to it. Empower the root on the New or Full Moon by anointing it with oil that is in accord with its nature. Speak to the root like a friend, and ask it what you want it to do in your life. Remember to go back every so often to speak to it, to maintain the relationship and to reanoint it with sacred oils.

Another way the green world can aid you in your development along all three rays is when you gather wood and craft a wand for each ray. Though we traditionally associate oak, ash, and thorn with the rays, each of us has an individual relationship with the rays, and your own personal associations might differ. In fact, they might surprise you.

When I first set out to craft my own wands, I originally sought only one wand, a replacement for a more traditional wand I had broken. The process symbolized a reforging of my will, as I was heading on a new path magickally and personally. In meditation I was given the day on which to cut my wand and was told what forest to enter in order to find the right wood. I brought an offering of milk, honey, and brandy and three silver coins for the spirit of the tree from which I would be taking the wood. I searched and searched, certain it would be from my power tree, the oak. I just wasn't sure if it would be red, white, or black oak. I kept coming back to a hemlock tree with a perfectly straight branch. It offered its branch to me, but asked only for a little of the liquid and one coin. I gave it, and then meditated. My guides from the Hidden Company told me to find two other trees. Their spirits would be calling me in these woods, and each of these trees would be my guide in the three rays. I soon found a bent red oak, which surprised me, as I thought if it was to be oak, then it would be white. Lastly I found a witch hazel with a crooked branch. Each received a coin and part of the offering. Each has become an aid in my own evolution along the three rays.

If and when you feel moved to do so, find three trees appropriate for you and craft three wands. Ask permission from the tree spirits. Make your offerings and harvest each branch. With a pocket knife, carefully strip its bark while still green and save the shavings. Let the wood dry over the next few months, then, when fully dry, oil the wand, pass it through consecrating incense, and bless it in ritual to attune to the appropriate ray. Some Witches anoint the wand with a drop of their own blood or sexual fluids, to truly attune it to their own body. Let the bark shavings dry and put them in a container of wood, paper, or, if necessary, glass, to create a talisman to contact your tree teacher. Consecrate the container in ritual. The wands will direct the energy of each ray, but the vessels, when held in meditation, will help you connect to the love and knowledge of each tree spirit and its deva and faery allies, no matter where you are. Decorate the container as desired. As time progresses, you can add dried leaves, seeds, nuts, and flowers from the same species of tree.

The highest magick of the second ray incorporates the knowledge and experience of prosperity and basic plant magick into the practice of a green lifestyle. Both herbal medicine and gardening encourage a deep relationship with the living spirits of the plants. The art and science of the second ray involve the practice of herbal medicine and the healing that occurs through the direct cultivation of plants. Many of the best herbalists I know grow their own plants, having a relationship with their medicine from the first shoots of the spring to the final medicinal product taken themselves or given to family and clients. I also know quite a few people who are not versed specifically in medicinal herbology but who have experienced powerful healing through the cultivation of a garden. The medicinal and spiritual properties are transferred directly from the plant without a medium, and change the gardener. Both herbal medicine and gardening require patience, love, knowledge, and experience. They are not armchair arts and sciences. You must get your hands dirty. You must touch the earth. You must find your love for the earth, for the green, and feel their love for you. In this work, our faery allies on all three levels are our best allies.

The famous Witch Sybil Leek advised budding Witches to drink a cup of red clover tea once a day, and that advice planted the seed to love and live with herbs in many future herbalists and priest/esses. It is one of the best things you can do for your overall health and well-being. While I do adore red clover, I recommend a more complex blend of herbs that are general tonics and nutritive for your health and aid in the prevention of disease and the build-up of stress. Place one tablespoon of this dried herbal mix in one cup of hot water, then cover and let steep for ten minutes. You can add a little honey to your liking and drink it often. Notice the difference in your overall health. As you progress, invite the spirits of these herbs into your life in other ways—in the garden, in the kitchen, in your meditations, visions, and dreams.

Witch's Tonic Tea
3 parts rose hips
1 part lemon balm
1 part red clover
1 part nettle
½ part licorice

Magick of the Crooked Line

The magick of the third ray is the most in alignment with humanity and the creatures of flesh and blood. It is the magick most natural to the majority of humans. It is in our blood, so to speak, for it is the magick most strongly associated with the blood.

In the Middle World, this quickening of the blood is felt through spells of romance, lust, and sexuality. This might seem strange and even contradictory to many, because the second ray is the ray of love, isn't it? It is, although, as has been emphasized, it is not sentimental love. While the powers of attraction, sex, and romance are closely associated with love in our culture, there are many forces we label love, many different expressions of love in our lives, and they are not all the same. Yet the energies of sexual attraction and romance operate on different frequencies than those of the love you feel when you are out in nature or the love you feel from the divine. There is a different magnetism, a different connecting force, operating. That is why it can be quite easy for many people to separate a desire for sex from a desire for love. Though these two often go together, sex and love are two separate things.

The magick of physical attraction is part of what makes us human. The forces that bring us together sexually are different from those that pollinate a flower. While the basis of so much of our magick is sex, and the life force that it expresses, humans express life force differently than plants and minerals do. And so much of our own culture and history, not to mention our gossips and scandals, revolves around romance, marriage, and sex. Sex is a basic desire and part of the human experience. Those who sublimate sex might find deep spiritual insight directing the energy elsewhere, but I think it is best to satisfy this desire, making it part of a healthy balance of life, the Frigg in the FFFF blessing, rather than letting it become a complex issue or obsession that needs to be dealt with later on in the magickal journey.

Sex and Romance Candle Spell

Candles can make excellent magickal tools for the third ray. Though at one time they were made from tallow, or animal fat, they still resonate with the animal nature of the third ray. Later development in candles gave us beeswax, another animal product. Other candles were made from spermaceti wax, from the sperm whale. Spermaceti is no longer used, with the general end of the whaling industry in the West. Most modern candles are made from petroleum products, from the fossil fuels of both plants and animals. While all types of candles are acceptable in magick, many Witches prefer to use beeswax whenever possible. Though expensive, beeswax candles are in many ways the most effective for magick and the best for our environment.

This very simple spell using a red taper candle usually is reserved just for sex, but also can be directed toward romance as well as physical satisfaction. Carve your name or initials into the candle with a pin, needle, or the edge of a blade you can wield safely. Traditionally one also would carve the male/Mars symbol and female/Venus symbol, to attract someone of the opposite sex (figure 11). If you are seeking someone of the same sex, use the appropriate Venus/Venus or Mars/Mars carving to suit your needs. Anoint the candle with your own saliva. Hold on to the candle tightly and think about the type of person you wish to attract. Imagine the experience you desire, be it sexual, romantic, or anything that suits your desires. Pour the images, feelings, desires, and words into the candle. When you feel the candle is "full" with your intention, light it and let it burn completely. If you can't let the candle safely burn completely in one sitting, snuff it out and then relight it.

FIGURE 11: MARS/VENUS, MARS/MARS, VENUS/VENUS SYMBOLS

The spell is not complete until the burning is done. You will attract the person and experience you desire.

Tradition says this spell always works simply to have sex, assuming you are not too choosy, but I've known quite a few people who have used it and ended up having a passionate affair with an attractive person. This spell doesn't tend to generate a lifelong mate or stable partnership, so if that is what you are looking for, you might want to try a different spell.

The discipline of the third ray deals with our kinship to our flesh and blood relatives, the animal world. Third ray magick involves the popular realm of totemic magick, working with the spirits of animals. Today many occultists say we each have a power animal, a totem or guide in the form of animal spirit that guides us in the spirit world and helps protect us. Some say the animal is a separate entity from us, a guardian. Others say it is part of, or attached to, our lower soul, and use terms such as the Fetch or Fetch Beast. Each animal spirit embodies a "medicine," an archetypal wisdom or learning that humans often forget (chart 12). Through the animal's actions, habitat, nature, and folklore, its medicine is revealed. Some animal spirit medicine teachings are simple and seem trite, such as dog embodying the medicine of loyalty. Yet in such simplicity, there is profound wisdom.

Animal	Magickal Properties
Ape	Intelligence, community
Ant	Industriousness, group consciousness, patience
Bat	Navigation, sound, darkness, Underworld, rebirth, initiation
Bear	Hibernation, balance, playfulness, power, hunting
Boar	Tenacity, strength, power, confrontation
Cat	Dreams, psychic power, instincts, self-indulgence
Crow	Sacred law, Underworld, Goddess
Dog	Loyalty, instinct, family, tracking
Dragonfly	Illusions, seeing truly
Eagle	Messenger, heavens, strength, divinity, air
Fox	Invisibility, camouflage, seasonal change, adaptability, protection, fire
Frog	Transformation, transition, song, sensitivity
Goose	Questing, travel, journey, speaking your mind, air
Horse	Power, travel, swiftness, healing
Jackal	Ancestor work, facing death, instincts, land, water

CHART 12: ANIMAL CORRESPONDENCES

Lion	Leadership, pride, courage, strength, fire
Lizard	Dreams, regeneration, rest, water, earth
Monkey	Cleverness, play, air
Rabbit	Fertility, facing fear, air, fire
Ram	Leadership, new beginnings, charging forward, fire
Salmon	Wisdom, eloquence, history, water, air
Skunk	Perception, reputation, community, acceptance
Snake	Change, healing, connection to the land, release, chakra power
Spider	Centeredness, writing, storytelling, new perception, weaving
Stag	Protection, awareness, leadership, earth
Wolf	Protection, clan, family, spiritual teacher, hunting, fire

CHART 12: ANIMAL CORRESPONDENCES (CONTINUED)

Our animal spirit is the one we embody most, though such notions give rise to fantasies where we do not see ourselves truly. Many people assume their animal totem is something majestic, powerful, or clever, and few want to claim kinship with the smaller, modest, yet equally profound totems. Others believe our totem is not who we are, but what we are learning to become. The animal embodies the medicine you need the most in this lifetime, but it often is not your natural inclination. The more you work with the animal spirit and allow it to guide you on the spiritual journey, the more you will embody its medicine, and people will associate the animal with you.

Animal magick involves communing with the spirits of these animals, invoking them in rituals and spells, and taking their form through the art of shapeshifting during shamanic trance. Many experience "faring forth" as their Fetch self, not seeing the animal in their journey, but becoming it.

I have had the pleasure of teaching magick to a wide range of people, from neophytes and dabblers to more experienced practitioners. One of the things that has amazed me time and time again is the vivid and direct experience people have when holding the intention to commune with animal spirits—more so than with plant magick, even when I have the herbs, oils, and essences out in the class, and more so than with stone magick, even if the students are surrounded by high-energy stones. The animal realm is the one we most easily align with and, in many ways, should be our first priority once the basics of ritual and magick are learned.

Animal Journey

Relax your body. Relax your mind. Open your heart. Feel the divine spark within. Engage the entire self for this working and prepare yourself for spiritual communion with the realm of the animal kin. Invoke the crooked line and call to the animal teachers and totems.

> *By the crooked line,*
> *I invoke the third ray.*
> *I invoke the yellow ray.*
> *I invoke the crooked ray of serpentine gold Witch fire.*
> *I invoke the ray of wisdom and cunning.*
>
> *By the power of divine wisdom,*
> *I seek to know, feel, and enact divine wisdom and cunning.*
> *I seek contact with the animal kin, the totems and teachers.*
> *I seek to know the wisdom of the beasts that humanity often forgets.*
> *Please teach me your ways,*
> *And show me your medicines.*
> *So mote it be.*

Conjure forth the World Tree of the three worlds. See its branches holding up the heavens. Feel the trunk as the axis around which the universe rotates in the world of space and time. Know that the roots dig deep into the Earth and Underworld. Feel the Tree illuminated by the crooked line. Slip through the veil of your mind and stand before the tree. Hold your intention to visit with an animal ally, an animal teacher.

The World Tree will open up for you. Its tunnels may spiral upward or downward, but the passageway will lead you to the animal kin that desires to work with you. Work with this animal ally. Let it show you its mysteries and its messages for you and the rest of your human kin. Remember its experience, and take it with you to the waking world. Feel the animal wisdom in your blood, your bones, your flesh and breath.

When you feel the experience is complete and the journey is over, bring your awareness completely back from the power of the crooked line. Ground and balance yourself as needed.

The highest form of third ray magick is working with living animals, building a relationship with the creatures of flesh and blood. Some who have devoted themselves to this lifestyle never practice animal magick, shapeshifting, or totemic work, yet are still profoundly wise. Those who both practice the magick and develop a relationship with our animal kin can experience an intense level of awareness and growth. Such a lifestyle can manifest as having a fully developed farm with animal breeding or simply having profound experiences with "pets" in our household. Any contact with the animal world, domestic or wild, is an opportunity for growth along the path of the third ray.

Other Magicks

While there are many other forms of magick to discuss, and many of these forms of magick do not fit in a specific place within our vision of the three rays, two major aspects of magickal work are healing and divination. Healing involves all three rays, for it requires balance between the three selves, as well as the three aspects of will, love, and wisdom. You could say the fundamental power of healing comes from the first ray, from the power to bless and curse, but unless you invoke the other two rays as a part of long-term healing work, you will not have long-lasting results.

Divination, on the other hand, is not simply an invocation of all three of these rays but is the ability to see their interplay in the three worlds, and translate such awareness into useful information. The information from a divination experience comes from the outside of the mandala, inward, looking at both the big picture and the details. The power of the first ray can fuel our psychic senses. Knowledge of the omens, and divination systems such as tarot, runes, or stones, aids us in the interpretation of divinatory information. Love connects our awareness not only to the intellect but also to the emotions behind our actions. Love helps us understand our connection to nature. It helps us see how nature is speaking to us through omens, portents, and sortilege devices. Alignment with all three rays leads to more balanced readings and psychic work.

The Callings

The blessings of the three rays also open us to magickal callings, vocations in harmony with the magick of each evolutionary path (chart 13). Though we may be called to a variety of careers, in both the magickal and mundane worlds, these callings, and the magicks associated with them, can be quite useful in understanding another aspect of our unfolding path, and how we unite will, love, and wisdom.

Ray	Underworld *Middle World*	Middle World *Lower World*	Upper World *Upper World*
First ray	Calling of Lapis	Calling of Devotion	Calling of Power
Second ray	Calling of Flora	Calling of the Healer	Calling of Dreams
Third ray	Calling of Fauna	Calling of the Bard	Calling of Knowledge

CHART 13: CALLINGS OF THE THREE RAYS

As with all things, the callings can be divided into areas of experience based on the three worlds. As the Underworld is the origin of life, each ray's magick is based on the "race" that is associated with that particular ray. The callings involve not just the spiritual races of angels, faeries, and totems, but also their physical manifestations through the stones, plants, and animals of the Middle World. Though the teachings of these entities were covered earlier in this chapter, the spiritual "call" one feels from them is quite powerful, and opens the door to a deeper level of wisdom, much as the gateway magick of power, prosperity, and attraction opens us to the first level of wisdom.

The work of minerals and metals is the Calling of Lapis, the stone conscious-ness of the Deep Earth. There are many who resonate so strongly with stones, gems, and crystals that they become charmed, fascinated, and sometimes totally absorbed in their vibration. This is also the case with those who are called to and are fascinated by the flora and the plant world. Those working in the vocations of the second ray can be charmed by the plants in their garden or get lost in the woods, playing in the consciousness that is the plant people's world. Those drawn to the animals of flesh and blood often feel less of a fascination and more of a kinship, a sense of tribe or family, with the creatures of the animal realm, and in truth animals are our closest relatives from the three races, for we are creatures of flesh and blood as well.

The callings of the Middle World represent vocations that deal with the community itself, and the interaction of the community with the world of spirits and the other races. Those on the first ray, serving the divine by drawing down divine will to be manifest upon Earth, often act as priests and priestesses, answering the call of devotion. These priestesses and priests are chosen by their patron gods, and commune between the gods and the people, acting as vessels for the gods' power and enacting their will in the Middle World. The second ray's calling blends well with the vocation of medicine, for it is the call to be a healer. Working with the plant realm leads from an understanding of magick to a clearer understanding of medicine, and how the two are related. The third ray's Middle World calling is more complex, for it is the sharing of human knowledge. The Cunning Ones, the inspired one, were associated at one time with the bardic arts. In Druidic tradition, the bard was the lowest of the ranks, as the first step in training was to be able to record, remember, recite, and create the poetry, music, history, and lore of the people. Those seeking the wisdom of the third way will start with knowledge, as knowledge can lead to wisdom if properly applied.

The callings of the Upper World have less to do with life and humanity and more to do with abstract principles, beyond the call of most humans. They are callings that often set us apart and mark us as decidedly different from those around us. The calling of the first ray is, unsurprisingly, the Calling of Power. It is not necessarily a sense of spiritual power, but rather the development of powerful abilities, what are called the siddhi in the Eastern traditions. It is the power to do things beyond the reach of normal humans, be it psychic skills to receive information and understanding about the past, present, and future, or the magickal power to effect change in the environment and the people around you. The Italian Strega lore of *The Gospel of Aradia* lists the Thirteen Powers of the Witch. They are said to be thirteen gifts from the Goddess, thirteen signs of a Witch, if you possess these abilities. The list has been adapted and modernized by practitioners, but basically outlines the following powers:

To use the power to bless friends and curse enemies.
To bring forth beauty, inner and outer.
To understand the secret signs of the hands, stars, cards, and omens.
To commune with animals and wild creatures.
To banish people, things, and even misfortune.
To cure disease and wounds of body, mind, heart, and soul.
To bring success in love.
To sense, conjure, converse, and command spirits.
To conjure good fortune.
To know and find hidden treasures and truths.
To understand the Voice of the Wind.
To predict and control the weather.
To possess the knowledge of transformation.

The Upper World calling of the second ray is the Calling of Dreams. It is the call of the artist and the creative individual, as well as that of the daydreamer. It is the exploration of things that are not, but might be. Some take this calling and manifest it as art, music, and poetry, sharing it with those of the Middle World. Many do not and instead explore fantasy and daydream, and through this may even commune with higher dimensions of consciousness, losing interest in the physical world of humanity.

The third ray's Upper World calling extends the Middle World calling of bardic skill. Rather than focus on retraining and sharing the collected lore of the people, it is the Calling of Knowledge. One is seeking knowledge of the higher, abstract realms, an understanding of the hows and whys of the universe, ultimately for the enlightenment that comes beyond personal development and self-realization.

While this system outlines three set of vocations for each world, our personal experience is not as cut-and-dried as it is in any system. We might find ourselves pulled by one ray's calling in the Middle World and a different ray's calling in the Lower or Upper World. The exploration of each makes us complete human beings, and for those of us on the cunning path of the Witch, we must ultimately master all three rays in all three worlds.

The Three Ray Cord

A powerful talisman used to evoke the power of all three rays in your life, and to become a touchstone when doing this work, is the three ray cord. Like a modern Witch's cord, it acts as a talisman to draw to you certain powers, and in this case, specifically the powers of the three rays. Though this charm can be worn like a belted cingulum around the robe, I usually make it smaller and wear it more like a necklace.

First, take three lengths of cord in a series of colors associated with the three rays. Red, blue, and yellow would be most appropriate, but you also could use white, red, and black, or gold, green, and black. I suggest using about four feet of each cord, so when you braid them together, you'll have about three feet, to bring the charm into alignment with the three measurements. Evoke the power of each ray into the appropriate cord. Feel the energy flow from your own hands into the cord, aligning it with the appropriate ray. Braid the cord as you would a traditional three-stringed braid. Feel the three powers supporting each other as you braid the cords together. Reflect on the connections between the rays and how each one is a necessary connection to the other, much like the three legs of a cauldron—it won't stand without all three.

Next, create three charm bags, one for each ray in the appropriate color. You can use actual charm bags sewn with drawstrings, which you can make yourself or find at many magickal supply shops. Or you can simply take a square of cloth, place the items of the cloth on it, gather the corners, and tie extra cord around the outside, creating a makeshift bag. Though the first method is probably more secure, I prefer the primal quality of the second, being someone not talented with a sewing needle. Though I prefer the second method, you might favor the drawstring approach if you want to be able to add to any of the bags or if you have any tools in the three bags that you want to be able to take out and put back in.

In the first ray charm bag, place a stone, mineral, or metal. Cleanse the stone of any unwanted energies and charge it with the power of the first ray. If you have a specific stone "totem" ally, then that would be appropriate. You also could place several stones you like and feel magickally connected to in the first bag. If you work strongly with the angelic realm, with specific angels that have traditional seals or sigils, then you could add a small talisman of the angelic seal in the bag as well. Cleanse and charge everything in this bag with the power and will of the first ray. In my own cord charm, I placed protection stones, particularly black tourmaline and smoky quartz, as they were two of the first stones I worked with in magick. I also have rose quartz and danburite in this pouch.

For the second charm bag, aligned with the second ray, place any herbs you feel an affinity for and charge them with the power of the second ray. If you have a particular "power herb" or plant spirit ally, place a portion of it in the bag. Whole roots can be used as a charm in this bag, oiled with an oil blend that is in harmony with the plant's purpose and intention. Roots can hold the energy and consciousness of a plant for a long time, and can be a charm themselves, commonly found in Witchcraft, Hoodoo, and conjure traditions. Though my own power plants are lemon balm, datura, and oak, the plants that wanted to be a part of this cord were the first two resins I ever used and continue to use daily, frankincense and myrrh.

For the third and final charm, aligned with the third ray, place in the bag anything related to your animal allies. If it is possible to use fur or feather that has been ethically, humanely, and legally gathered, then do so. Various representations of the animal also can be used, such as a photograph or a charm carved from stone or made from clay. My own bag contains wolf hair, one of the first totem animals I worked with in magick. As with the previous bags, charge this one with the energy of its ray.

When you are ready, tie the three bags, evenly spaced, onto the cord. Then you can hang the cord from your neck like a lamen or tie it around your waist like a belt. Or you can knot the ends and wear it as a necklace. Wear it when doing work with the three rays, to align yourself to the threefold power.

You can work with other substances and tools to align with the three rays, creating charms and relics, to combine the three rays or work with an individual ray. Objects of power can be created from stone, in particular meteorite for the red ray; wood, amber, and jet for the blue ray; and bone for the yellow ray.

Each of the three rays provides a gateway magick into the mysteries. Your need or desire for protection, prosperity, or love can open the way. Each ray contains a discipline of more formal and complex magick, encoded with correspondences. Witches often choose to specialize in the use of stone magick, plant magick, or animal magick. Lastly, each ray provides a way of life, working with the traditions of alchemy and the transformations of minerals and metals, working deeply with plant medicine in the garden, or working with animals on the farm.

Though many of us are called to lifestyles and options entirely off the map of the three rays, this system provides a powerful framework to evaluate the decisions we make in our magick, disciplines, and lifestyle, helping us figure out if our work is in harmony with our own will, love, and wisdom. The three rays lead to a greater understanding of our process of evolution and enlightenment and, in the end, lead us to the "greater" magick of the mysteries, of the resurrection described in the Descent of the Goddess. Our resurrection comes in three forms: the transmigration of the soul (or souls) from life to life, the rebirth we undergo during initiation, and the rebirth we undergo when we craft our three souls and unite power, love, and wisdom and become one of the Mighty Dead.

PART THREE:
PEACE
OF THE
MYSTERIES

CHAPTER SEVEN:
THE THREE JOURNEYS

Of all the trees that grow so fair, Old England to adorn, Greater are none beneath the Sun, Than Oak, and Ash and Thorn.—"A Tree Song" by Rudyard Kipling

The three rays extend forward into the three worlds, creating a ninefold plot of reality. Exploring each realm grants you access to a different level of power, love, and wisdom that cannot be put into words but only experienced. The three rays in the Underworld resonate with the three threads, each leading to a different type of wisdom, and resonate with one of the three sacred wells in our mythology. In the Middle World, the three rays bring us to visions of the Holy Powers, forces that integrate the Middle World with the heavens and depths. And the three rays in the Upper World grant us a vision of the different sources of stellar fire.

Once you have opened the gates of magick for each ray, and found allies on the path, you are ready to journey deeper into the realms and their mysteries.

The Journeys of the Underworld

The journeys of the Underworld revolve around the manifestation of the rays as three threads. Just as the colors of the rays transform as they journey through the three worlds, so do the natures of the rays transform. They thin and unwind into almost invisible presences, into threads that are part of the fabric of reality but are thin lines that go unseen by most. The threads turn white, red, and black, echoing both the colors classically associated with the triple goddess and the stages of alchemical transformation, though in alchemy the order usually is black, white, and red. These threads are secret links to the Cauldron of Regeneration itself, in the heart of the Underworld. Each one links us to a different aspect of the mysteries.

Part of my later workings with the three ray vision showed me that each of these threads seems to lead to a different well, and I took the names of these wells from Norse mythology. While mythology gives us three potential different locations for each of the wells, as each has a different nature, for the purpose of this work we'll look at these specific wells as primal cauldrons, calderas/kalderas of the spirit world. They all are aspects of the first cauldron, the one in the heart of the Underworld. All are mythically one cauldron, the one in the heart of Annwn, the Underworld. We just perceive them in different places, call them different names, and work with the different natures of their "waters."

The thread of the third ray is the one most easily accessible to us. The naturally golden third ray manifests as the red of blood in the Middle World. That is the same color that imbues its mystic thread. The red thread is the thread of our ancestors. It is scarlet red, as it is the color of blood. The red thread leads us to ancestral wisdom, granting us intuitive knowledge that is passed on to us from those who came before. This strand is first found in the lore of our people. The rituals, myths, beliefs, and practices we inherit from our blood relatives and our culture provide the foundation. They are the first clues to this ancestral wisdom. Through their use, we can make contact with spiritual ancestral allies, those entities in our blood, spiritual tradition, or overarching culture who will provide information and insight into our spiritual practices and practical lives. The red thread leads us through the gates of past knowledge to the Well of Wisdom, the collective vessel of ancestral wisdom. This is also known as the Well of Mimir, of Mímisbrunnr, of Memories. Mimir is a god from Norse mythology who originally guarded this Well of Wisdom. He was beheaded in the war between the Aesir and Vanir gods, and the Aesir god Odin received the head, preserved it with herbs and magick, and consulted it for wisdom and oracular divination. Odin himself sacrificed one eye for a single drink from this well.

The thread of the second ray is a difficult path. The naturally blue ray transforms into the greenery of nature in the Middle World, but its thread becomes black in the Underworld. The black thread leads us to knowledge through the path of the ordeal, the traumatic experience that produces earned wisdom. Though we see the faeries of the Underworld as beloved kin, they also represent a hard path. Faery myth is filled with trickery, curses, and abductions, poetic expressions of the darker side of nature. Initiations into magick often are ordeals, facing life and death, and it is the graveness of the situation that utterly transforms you. Wisdom found in the face of hardship and danger is much more tangible than the knowledge found in books or philosophical daydreaming. The black thread of earned knowledge leads through the faery realm to the depths of the Underworld, to the Seething Cauldron or Roaring Kettle, Hvergelmir. This well is the source of many of the rivers of creation, and some associate it with Nidhogg. Nidhogg is the serpent or dragon that lives in the roots of the World Tree, feeding upon the roots and damaging the Tree itself. With associations of both creation through the rivers and destruction as a seething vessel near the home of a destructive dragon, this well truly is a force of change, and potentially healing.

The first ray seemingly is the easiest to experience once you make a connection to it, but it is the most elusive and difficult to actually find. The natural red ray manifests in the Middle World as the king of the metals, gold, but it becomes pure white as it winds into a thread. The white or silver thread is the line of spiritual knowledge. This is information that comes from direct gnosis, containing new insights previously unknown. The gift of the white thread is freely given, unlike the knowledge from the ordeal that must be earned through hardship. Some say it is the mystery of the white bones, the bones not just of our own ancestors but also of the Earth, the rock and stone and hills that hold the divine patterns that predate us. The white thread leads us to the beginning of creation, to the Well of Wyrd, the Well of Fate, also known as Urdarbrunnr. This well is named for Urd, one of the Norns, or fates, of Norse mythology. The three sisters take water from this well and feed the World Tree so its branches will not rot, repairing the damage caused by the various creatures that live within the Tree. The white thread and the Well of Wyrd reveal the connections between people, places, and the past, present, and future. The white thread reveals the consequences of what has come before, and is a direct line to the creative powers of the universe.

The three rays have been associated with the folk teachings in Witchcraft of three sacred trees. Though the trees themselves vary in different climates and cultures, they are embodiments of the sacred pillars found in many traditions, with the doorway or threshold guardian opening and closing the way between the pillars. The most popular and well known of these trios, particularly in modern Witchcraft, is the oak, ash, and thorn trees. Although the three trees work together in the pagan spiritual teachings, their specific associations with the three rays are tenuous at best, as each tree could be related to any of the rays.

In my own vision of the rays, the oak is associated with the first ray, as a tree that is strong, rooted, and unbending. Though its classic planetary association is with Jupiter, and Jupiter's Qabalistic sephira, Chesed, is on the Pillar of Mercy and thus would be associated with the second ray, I still feel the overall power of oak from folk tradition aligns best with the first ray. It reaches up and connects us with the heavens and what can be perceived as the angelic powers. Like the first line, the oak is unyielding. It maintains its rigidity, even sometimes to its own detriment, when facing a storm more powerful than its roots.

The ash tree is aligned with the power of the second ray, the bent line. In the northern traditions of Saxon and Norse paganism, the ash usually is seen as the World Tree, the cosmic axis of Yggdrasil. Though the ash is not associated with the faery races of the second ray in particular, modern systems have corresponded its ogham symbol, Nion, with the planet Neptune, named for the Roman god of the sea (figure 12). In modern Hermetic Qabalah that includes the outer planets, the sephira Chokmah also is aligned with Neptune, and Chokmah is at the top of the Pillar of Mercy, the Qabalistic pillar corresponding to our second ray. Ash trees are quite resistant to water and are used to make boats and oars. The wood is both tough and elastic, making it quite versatile in its use, particularly for weapons, as it yields a good bow, what could be considered a "bent" line. The ash is sacred to the Welsh god Gwydion as well as to the Norse god Odin. Gwydion is said to fashion wands from ash, and while his role and origin are unclear —deity, deified ancestor, Mighty Dead, or faery being—he sometimes is considered to be the prince of the Tylwyth Teg, or "Fair Folk," of Welsh cosmology.

OAK   ASH   HAWTHORN   BLACKTHORN

FIGURE 12: OGHAM OF OAK, ASH, HAWTHORN, AND BLACKTHORN

The thorn tree, be it the white hawthorn or the dark blackthorn, is not as massive as the oak and ash, and although it is not often considered a World Tree, it is typically associated with faery lands and the Otherworld. The thorn stands between the two taller trees, like a barrier and gateway. Though it has direct associations with the faery races, it has a dual nature, making it perfect for alignment with the crooked ray. Both thorn trees have associations with Witchcraft. The white and black varieties of thorn can bring both blessings and curses. Though in general whitethorn is considered "good" and blackthorn is considered "bad" or at least baneful, both trees have sharp spikes. Admittedly, the blackthorns are larger and more dangerous. Both types yield fruits. The hawthorn is more medicinal, creating a tonic for the heart from the red berries, but the blackthorn produces the sloe used in the magickal and warming drink sloe gin. I work with the dual nature of the thorn tree, standing between oak and ash, to align with the third ray of wisdom and cunning.

Oak, ash, and thorn collectively comprise a gateway into the Otherworld in Celtic tradition, what we might think of as the Underworld, a realm of guides and totems where wisdom is available if we simply know how to ask for it and listen.

Underworld Journey to the Three Threads

Relax your body. Relax your mind. Open your heart. Feel the divine spark within. Engage the entire self for this working, and prepare yourself for spiritual communion with the realm of the Underworld, to trace the three threads of fate and find which thread presents itself as a blessing or challenge for you. Invoke the Fates and their mysteries.

> *By the straight line and the white thread,*
> *By the crooked line and the red thread,*
> *By the bent line and the black thread,*
> *I invoke the Three Who Are One.*
> *I invoke the Ladies Three of spirit, flesh, and void .*
> *I invoke the Ladies Three of bone, blood, and essence.*
> *I invoke the Ladies Three of silver, crimson, and jet.*
> *By the divine will, wisdom, and love,*
> *I seek to know your mysteries and learn the way of the loom.*
> *I seek to know your mysteries and weave my own fate.*
> *I seek to know your mysteries and find the thread that will lead me*
> *Into and out of the labyrinth.*
> *Please show me the way.*
> *Blessed be.*

Conjure forth the World Tree of the three worlds. See its branches holding up the heavens. Feel the trunk as the axis around which the universe rotates in the world of space and time. Know that the roots dig deep into the Earth and Underworld. Perhaps the gateway is not one tree, but rather the triune doorway of oak, ash, and thorn. Feel the gateway illuminated with the energies of the three rays. Hold your intention to visit the Underworld.

The gateway opens for you. Perhaps one of your allies from the spirit realms, such as an animal guide, will be there to guide you. Descend into the depths. Perhaps the allies of the faery or angelic realm will work with you on the journey. Travel deeper into the land below, until you find the crossroads of the three ways.

There at the crossroads, waiting for you, is the Goddess of Fate. She can manifest in many forms, perhaps as a single weaver, of any age and any shape, or as a triune goddess, with many ages and shapes and colors. Generally she appears in the colors of the three threads: white, red, and black. There at the crossroads, introduce yourself, if you have not met her gaze before. She already knows you, as she knows all things.

Speak to the Goddess of Fate. Depending on her aspect, she will give you one of the three threads. Will she give you the white thread of gnosis, of direct knowing with no price to pay? With the white thread, you will walk the way of divine will and power, the straight line of the Underworld. This path simply leads to the Well of Fate, where you may gather knowledge of what was, what is, and what will be.

Will the Goddess of Fate give you the red thread of ancestral wisdom, where you may have to commune with or redeem your own ancestors of blood? With the red thread, you will walk the way of wisdom and cunning, the crooked path of the Underworld. This path leads to the Well of Wisdom, the wisdom of those who have come before.

Will the Goddess of Fate give you the black thread of ordeal, where you might have to face trauma and darkness? With the black thread, you walk the way of divine love and trust, the bent line of the Underworld. This path leads to the Seething Cauldron, that which destroys in order to create.

Take the thread you have been given. Follow the thread on its appropriate path. Seek out the mysteries and wisdom only you can unlock at this place and time. Feel the power of the Fates awaken and activate within you.

The journey will culminate with scrying into the appropriate well or cauldron, gazing upon the otherworldly water. Scry into the water. Let its secrets open the way for you. In the vision, you will be given a glyph, a bind rune, or some other symbol. This symbol will be the direct connection to the power that returns with you from the world below. Memorize the symbol now. Affirm that you will remember it upon returning to the land of the waking.

Follow the path up and out of the Underworld. Your path may take you back to the crossroads, back to the lady of fate, or return you via another route. Return through the gateway of the tree, or the three trees of oak, ash, and thorn. Carve your symbol into the bark of one of the trees, if you feel moved to do so. With this action, you root and ground the Underworld power in the land of flesh and blood, breath and bone, cycle, season, and direction.

When you feel the experience is complete and the journey is over, bring your awareness completely back from the power of the Underworld. Ground and balance yourself as needed. You can make a physical talisman of the symbol you retrieved.

The Journeys of the Middle World

The Middle World journeys are not quite as perilous as those of the Underworld. Generally, they do not confer much information from spiritual contacts. They do, however, help you make connections to the power of the three rays, and aid in strengthening your connections between the Middle World and the realms above and below.

Each of the Middle World journeys is an experience that leads to the Garden of the Gods, the primal time and place of connection where the three rays find harmony. The vision of the first ray in the Middle World is the alchemist's ladder. It is the process of digging up the sacred metals of the seven planets, exposing them to the forces of time and space in the Middle World, and transmuting each until we discover the Philosopher's Stone and the alchemist's True Gold, within and without. Does this confer enlightenment by itself, or immortality? Not necessarily, but it is a vision that gives us a glimpse into this state of consciousness. It opens a potential path.

The Middle World vision of the second ray provides similar insight, but from the perspective of nature and the faery races. Through this vision you find the Emerald Heart of the Earth. You find its light bubbling up like a well or fountain. Occultists sometimes refer to the source of this fountain of light as the Laboratory of the Holy Spirit rather than the Emerald Heart. The fountain of earthlight also can be referred to as Hecate's Fountain, and plays a prominent role in the mysteries of the vortices. Wherever the lines of light cross in a sacred space, the fountain may rise up and swirling bent lines flow off from the vortex created. The vision of this light, and its source, restores our consciousness with that of the plants and faery races of this planet.

The last vision, the Middle World vision of the third ray, brings us to the Holy Blood of the Living Creatures. As in stories of Adam naming the animals and the Garden of Eden, this is a vision of the primal time when animals and humans were one. Humans did not fear animals, and animals did not fear humans. There was an understanding among us all. Our vision of these creatures helps us understand where we have been as a race and where we are going now.

The three individual parts of this vision can be divided and done separately as three distinct shorter workings or combined into a triple working with three separate parts.

Visions of the Great Between

Relax your body. Relax your mind. Open your heart. Feel the divine spark within. Engage the entire self for this working, and prepare yourself for spiritual communion with the realm of the Middle World, the land between and the sacred vision of all things around you. Invoke the spirit of the place, the genius loci, of where you are, for the spirit of the place will be both guardian and guide, the spirit who opens you to the Visions of the Great Between. As you make this invocation, it is appropriate to make an offering to the guardian of the land, such as milk and honey, bread, wine, tobacco, cornmeal, or chocolate. Say:

> *By the straight line, I invoke the power of the Heavenly Ladder,*
> *Seven metals, steven steps leading to perfected gold.*
> *By the bent line, I invoke the power of the Emerald Heart.*
> *May the awenyddion reveal the fallen stone within the rising fountain.*
> *By the crooked line, I invoke the power of the Holy Blood.*
> *May the sacred creatures of fang and fur, feather and claw, fin and scale,*
> *Open us to their wisdom.*
> *By the Three Who Are One, I call upon the spirit of this place and time.*
> *I call upon the spirit of the land and all that lies between.*
> *I ask the guardian of the gate to open the way and let me pass.*
> *May there always be peace between us.*
> *Blessed be.*

Conjure forth the World Tree of the three worlds. See its branches holding up the heavens. Feel the trunk as the axis around which the universe rotates in the world of space and time. Know that the roots dig deep into the Earth and Underworld. Perhaps the gateway is not one tree, but rather the triune doorway of oak, ash, and thorn. Feel the gateway illuminated with the energies of the three rays. Hold your intention to visit the realm between, just beyond the edges of what we normally perceive.

The gateway opens for you. You step through and into a world not unlike the realm of space and time you normally inhabit. Wherever you were when you began this journey, you are still there, but simply in the spirit double of the place. Everything glows with an otherworldly light, revealing its true nature and spirit, revealing its essence. You are seeing the etheric forms that support the material world, and all the spirits and powers that hover at the edge of our awareness, at the periphery of our consciousness.

Invoke the power of the first ray, the straight line. Feel the presence of divine will and power. Then feel yourself slowly sinking into the land. You are descending not into the Underworld but into the realm between, neither above nor below, yet mingling with the soil, the minerals, and the metals. You feel as if you can "swim" through the layers of the Earth, and you feel a strong pull, a sense of gravity or magnetism, leading you toward the seven sacred metals. There in the womb of the Earth you have a vision of the seven sacred metals.

You perceive the power of lead deepest within the Earth. Lead is the manifestation of Saturn within the Earth, heavy and dark. It is the power of karma and balancing out the actions of our past. It is the weight we cannot escape unless we transform it. It is the metal of cursing tablets and shackles, but it also is the softest, most pliable, and easiest to affect with your magick. Do not fear the lead.

You perceive the power of tin within the land. Tin is the manifestation of Jupiter within the Earth, lighter and looking like silver, yet more brittle when cooled. It sometimes is known as "white lead." It works best in alloys rather than on its own. Tin teaches us to work with others rather than stand alone. Tin also is the power of greed and its opposing virtue, generosity. Feel the power of tin.

You perceive the power of iron, forming veins within the ground. Iron is the manifestation of Mars within the Earth. The oxide of iron is like the blood of the Earth. It resonates with the blood of living creatures and with the magnetic field of the Earth herself, for iron tools are the instruments most likely to shed blood and make the Earth run red. Iron wounds but also protects. It separates us from that which would do us harm. Respect the power of iron.

You perceive the power of copper dwelling in the land. Copper is the manifestation of Venus within the Earth, a rosy metal tarnishing to green, like the green of vegetation as it decays. Copper conducts power and can be crafted into many beautiful and functional tools, working well on its own and with other metals. Copper is the power of attraction and love. It is reflective and the first of the beautiful metals. Experience the power of copper.

You experience the power of quicksilver, of mercury, trapped in the solid rock. Quicksilver is the manifestation of Mercury in the Earth. This silver fluid flows freely yet often remains contained within the land. No container can hold it for long, as it changes and adapts and runs when you try to catch it. Toxic to humans yet one of the holy powers of the land, quicksilver teaches us the sacredness and danger of our words and thoughts flowing and running from us. Flow with the power of quicksilver.

You experience the power of silver, of the metallic lunar light within the depths. Silver is the manifestation of the Moon within the Earth, reflective and solid. Silver reflects both matter and spirit. It enhances psychic power and conducts many forms of energy. Silver moves with the tides of life within us and around us, pulled by the call of the Moon Lady. Feel the tides of silver.

You experience the power of gold, the light within the land. Gold is the manifestation of the Sun within the Earth. It is the king of all metals, the enlightened mineral toward which all others seek to evolve. It is ruler and the Child of Promise and Light. Gold grants both physical and mystical might, health and inspiration, wealth and blessings in all things. Feel the power of gold, of the royal metal.

The seven metals arrange themselves in a pattern before you, taking the shape of a ladder. The alchemical metals and their transformative process link the depths of the Underworld to the height of the heavens, but you realize that it is here, between, in the world of space and time, that they really can transform. If the seven metals are not transmuted, worked with by human hands, by magicians and alchemists, then they simply remain inert in the land. Their secret power awakens only in the Middle World, in the realm of space, time, and process. Only through transformation can the metals connect the depths the Underworld with the heart of the heavens.

***

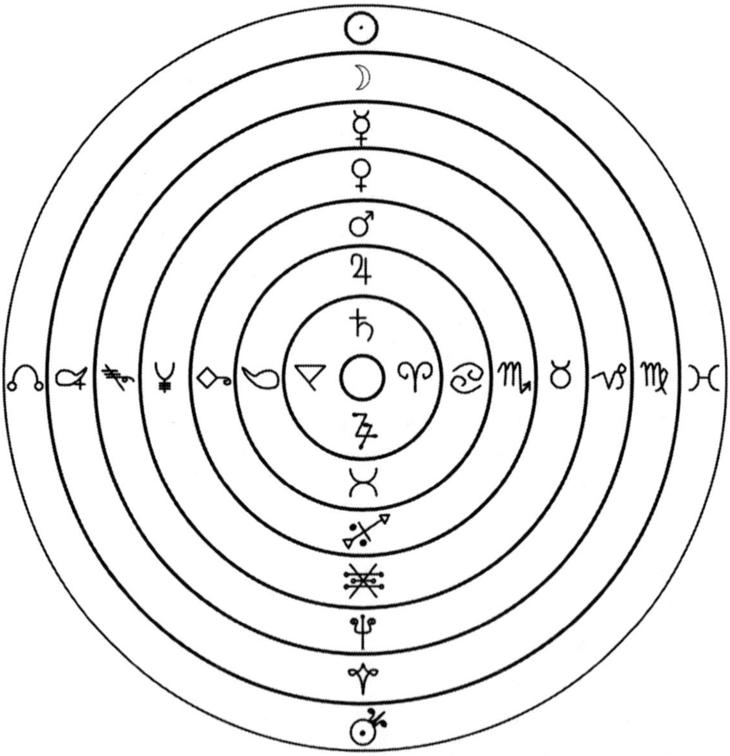

FIGURE 13: ALCHEMICAL SIGILS

With the vision of the first ray complete, invoke the power of the second ray, the bent line. Feel the power of the bent line open to you. The strange magnetic pull takes you to a new place, a new land, in harmony with the forces of the second ray yet still in the Middle World, the land between.

You find yourself on the surface of the land, at a nexus point, a node where many sacred lines of force meet, creating and framing a vortex of energy rising from the depths and reaching the heavens. The energy vortex is like a fountain of light, like an immense water fountain, but instead of shooting water it spurts up the life force of the planet. It is strange and beautiful. It is hypnotic and holy. You are drawn to its presence. Feel yourself enter the fountain of light. Feel the swirling and pulsing movements up and down and spinning around. If the land finds you worthy and ready, then you will be drawn into the center of the vortex. You will be given access to the Laboratory of the Holy Spirit and shown the Emerald Heart of the Earth, the pulsing green stone of love (figure 14). Many say the green heart fell from the brow of an angel and was carved into the Holy Cup of the Grail.

FIGURE 14: HEART OF THE EARTH

Yet it is still whole and perfect within the Heart of the Earth, and all vortices lead to the same green heart. The loving heart reveals its presence to you, and you find yourself merged with the one heart with the land. There is no separation between you and the land, the soil, the plants, animals, oceans, and air. You are part of a greater whole. Be one with the Heart of the Earth.

When the process is complete, you gradually resume your individuality from the Heart of the Earth, as if the heart is giving birth to you in the world again. Reborn, you find your center and maintain a sense of connection to the land.

* * *

When the vision of the second ray is done, invoke the power of the third ray. The magnetic pull of the planet brings you to an otherworldly garden, like the fabled Eden of Judeo-Christian myth or the pagan paradise of Hesperides or Avalon. Time and space shift around you until you find yourself in the Garden. There you find the World Tree you are familiar with, or the trinity of oak, ash and thorn. Around the trees is every manner of creature you can imagine. All those of the animal kingdom are waiting for you.

In the center of the garden you are approached by all the creatures of the world. As each one approaches you, individually and in groups, you feel your blood resonate and vibrate in harmony with their blood, like different notes on the same cosmic piano, each contributing to the Song of the Universe. You are approached by the animal kingdom's consciousness in the Great Chain of Being and realize that, rather than being progressive links on the chain, we all are like notes in a chord, each equal and each different.

You gaze into a pool in the garden and see among the rippling waves the tiniest of sea creatures, our primordial ancestors who come from the single cells of the First Mothers. They are followed by all manner of creatures from the depths, the jellyfish, crustaceans, squids, octopuses, and shellfish. You see all sorts and colors of fish swimming in the pool. You see the boned fish and the mighty sharks and rays. You see massive swimmers and tiny gliders on the waves.

You begin to notice all the insects and arachnids on the vegetation around you. One by one they become more visible, coming out of their hiding holes and making an appearance. First come the beetles, followed by the spiders, scorpions, and ants. Next are the flying insects, the fruitflies and mayflies, mosquitos, stinging wasps and hornets, and moths, then the bees and butterflies.

At the edge of the pool you are approached by the amphibians, the water and air breathers. Soon after come the reptiles, some without legs, like the serpents, and others with legs, like the lizards.

You are approached by the races of birds, winged and feathered, large and small. In particular you notice the eagle, crow, owl, dove, swan, vulture, and wren.

You are approached by the four-legged mammals from around the world. Many are furry and connected to the land. Some are large and powerful. Others are tiny and inconspicuous. Some have horns. Some have leathery skin. Some dig. Some climb.

You are approached by the two-legged creatures, which are most like humans. You see the primates—monkeys, gorillas, orangutans, and chimpanzees—from the African continent. You see a wisdom in their eyes beyond what most of us think is possible in the animal world.

You gaze back into the pool of water and see the air-breathing sea dwellers, the dolphins and whales. You see the sea lions, porpoises, and penguins. You feel their breath and hear their song.

You see humanity—all races, all lands, all evolutions.

You feel the power of the animal realm all around you and within you, and at this point in time and space, all is at peace, all is in harmony. You feel the flow of the Holy Blood of the Living Creatures within you as well, and know that, despite all appearances, it is not only in this moment but in all moments that the natural world is in harmony and at peace. In the Middle World, the cycle of life, birth, and death is holy. The roles of the hunter and the hunted are in harmony.

Remember your three visions. Feel their power, love, and wisdom. Carry them in your heart and return to the land of your own flesh and blood, breath, and bone. Return to the cycles, seasons, and directions supported by this etheric world of perfection.

When you feel the experience is complete and the journey is over, bring your awareness completely back from the power of the Middle World. Ground and balance yourself as needed.

The Journeys of the Upper World

Our travels to the Upper World, to see the vision of the stars, take us beyond the realms of earthly concerns or Underworld initiation. Though we travel to the heavens, in many ways we return to the heart of the cauldron, the start of time and space, where all things began. The highest of the heavens leads us to the darkest depths of the cauldron. There is no knowledge here. There are no words here. It is simply a return to the source of the three rays as embodied by a star of red fire, a star of blue fire, and a star of golden yellow fire. The hearts of these stars reveal not only our will, love, and wisdom, but also the will, love, and wisdom of creation.

Journey to the Upper World

Relax your body. Relax your mind. Open your heart. Feel the divine spark within. Engage the entire self for this working, and prepare yourself for spiritual communion with the realm of the Upper World, the land above and the sacred vision of Heaven. Invoke the spirit of the stars to open the gates of Heaven. Then speak this invocation:

> *By the straight line, I invoke the power of the red star,*
> *Burning brightly with power and will.*
> *By the bent line, I invoke the power of the blue star,*
> *Icy fire of love and trust.*
> *By the crooked line, I invoke the power of the golden star,*
> *Royal lantern held in the body of the hermit Prometheus Luciferio.*
> *May the three royal eyes gaze upon me, within me, and through me,*
> *Never averting their light.*
> *Now until the end of time.*
> *So mote it be.*

Conjure forth the World Tree of the three worlds. See its branches holding up the heavens. Feel the trunk as the axis around which the universe rotates in the world of space and time. Know that the roots dig deep into the Earth and Underworld. Perhaps the gateway is not one tree, but rather the triune doorway of oak, ash, and thorn. Feel the gateway illuminated with the energies of the three rays. Hold your intention to visit the realm above, to dwell with the stars in the branches of the Tree.

Climb the Tree of the World, the One Tree that is everywhere and nowhere. Climb it with all your earthly power until there is no further to go. With your unearthly power, the supernatural will of the Witch that resides within you, will yourself to move higher, to the blackest heavens of the deepest space beyond the known heavens. Search for the beginning of the beginning, the fires before fires burned, and the light that shone before darkness ever was.

Call out to the first of the three fires:

> *By the straight line of will and power,*
> *By the red eye of the bull and the fallen pride of angels,*
> *I open the way to Aldebaran, red giant of the Seven Sisters.*
> *Alpha Tauri, shine brightly upon me.*

In the black void of space, see the red fire, the red star. Reach through the red power of Mars, through the red-orange power of Aldebaran, to the light and power beyond all that is known. Reach into the red fire of divine will and become one with it. Commune with the divine will of the cosmos, and know your own True Will within the cosmic pattern.

Draw the fire of the red star within you, and feel it take hold within your right eye. See your will clearly in the world.

Call out to the second of the three fires:

By the bent line of love and trust,
By the blue-white lyre of Orpheus and the Song of Creation, the Oran Mór,
I open the way to Vega, Vultur Cadens, light and judge of Heaven.
Alpha Lyrae, shine brightly upon me.

In the black void of space, see the blue fire, the blue star. Reach through the power of blue-green Venus, through the blue-white power of Vega, to the light and power beyond all that is known. Reach into the blue fire of divine love and become one with it. Commune with the divine love of the cosmos, and feel your own Perfect Love within the cosmic pattern.

Draw the fire of the blue star within you, and feel it take hold within your left eye. See the world through the eye of Perfect Love.

Call out to the third of the three fires:

By the crooked line of wisdom and cunning,
By the golden yellow of the Guardian Bear,
I open the way to Arcturus, Alchameth, ruler of the sky.
Alpha Bootes, shine brightly upon me.

In the black void of space, see the yellow fire, the yellow star. Reach through the power of orange Mercury, through the yellow power of Arcturus, to the light and power beyond all that is known. Reach into the golden fire of divine wisdom and become one with it. Commune with the divine wisdom of the cosmos, and feel your own knowledge and wisdom come into bloom within the cosmic pattern.

Draw the fire of the golden star within you, and feel it take hold within your brow, the third eye. See the world through the eye of wisdom and cunning.

Remember the light of the three stars (figures 15 and 16). Feel them illuminating your brow and your eyes, being a triple-eyed creature, seeing truly now, as the divine sees you. Bring the stars back into the cauldron of your skull, of inspiration. Ground their light in your vision and in your bones.

When you feel the experience is complete and the journey is over, bring your awareness completely back from the power of the Upper World. Ground and balance yourself as needed.

Say:
The three cauldrons are a mystery,
For their nature is of the Underworld,
Yet at times they can appear in the worlds above.
The Well of Wisdom can be found in the Land of Space and Time.
The Well of Wyrd can be found among the gods in Heaven.
But the Seething Well is always found in the Great Below.

The three treasures are a mystery,
For their nature is of the Middle World,
Yet at times they can appear in the Worlds Above and Below.
The Alchemist's Gold can unlock the doors to Heaven.
The Emerald Heart can be found in the depths of Hell.

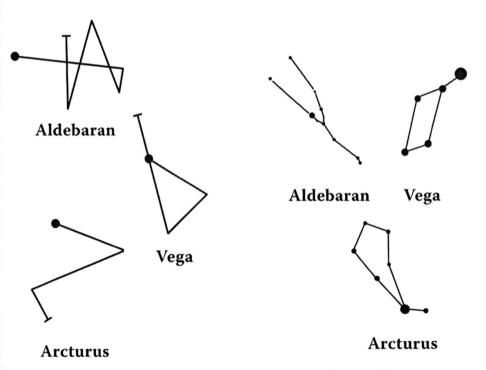

Aldebaran

Vega

Arcturus

Aldebaran   **Vega**

Arcturus

FIGURE 15:
SIGILS OF THE THREE STARS

FIGURE 16:
THREE CONSTELLATIONS OF THE STARS

PART THREE: PEACE OF THE MYSTERIES

But the Holy Blood of Living Creatures is always found in the Great Between.

The three stars are a mystery,
For their nature is of the Upper World,
Yet at times they can appear in the Worlds Below.
The blue star can be found in the heart of the Underworld.
The golden star can be found in the Paradise Lost Around Us.
But the red star is always found in the Great Above.

The red star manifests as Aldebaran and is mediated by Mars.
The blue star manifests as Vega and is mediated by Venus.
The golden yellow star manifests as Arcturus and is mediated by Mercury.
The triune planets are surrounded by the elder parents of Saturn and Jupiter
And the younger parents of the Moon and the Sun.
See through the three eyes of Cruithear, CeliCed, and Dryghten.
So mote it be!

CHAPTER EIGHT: THREE PATHS OF INITIATORY WISDOM

Initiation is like vaccination: if it takes, there is an unmistakable reaction. —Dion Fortune, "Ceremonial Magic Unveiled," in the *Occult Gazette,* January 1933

The most important part of the magick of the three rays is that each ray is an initiatory path, a soul's calling to experience the mysteries. Working with the allies and developing magickal and visionary skills all are steps on these lifelong paths. The vision of the three rays provides a map for understanding the path of your three souls that move as one, and leads to a greater understanding of others on the Witch's path. By keeping these paths in mind and observing your Witch kin, you might gain a better understanding of their paths, powers, blessings, and hardships.

The three rays express three distinct forms of Witch, shaman, or magician. Though there are many more expressions to the magickal practitioner, these are the ones most in alignment with our work in the realm of will, love, and wisdom. Though humans walk the third path, the crooked path, and must choose love and power in order to have wisdom bloom within them, we might take a path to specialize in one of the other two branches and their development in humanity, revealing particular mysteries.

The King's Path

The first ray is the straight road of the king's path. It is the path of service to the community, found in the tradition of sacred kings and warriors. It is for those who walk a path of challenge and often hardship, and those who sacrifice self for others in divine exchange. It is the path of those who are in communion with the land as it intersects with humanity, as embodied by the dragon lines and straight tracks at sacred sites, places where communities gather in seasonal celebration.

Classically, the sacred king was one who mediated the energies of the gods for the people. The sacred kings were priest-kings, and were considered divine embodiments. We see such a tradition in the pharaohs of Egypt. In the Celtic sacred king traditions, the king mediated the energy of the Goddess of the Land, as exemplified in the saying "The king and the land are one." The king was sacrificed, in reality, by proxy or in effigy, depending on the time period, to renew the land and the people's relationship with it. If the community was suffering, if the crops would not grow, if there was illness or corruption throughout the land, then the cause was the king's relationship with the Goddess. Our tales of the Arthurian tragedy are based on this mystic teaching. The land transforms from noble Camelot to the Wasteland because of the imbalanced relationship Arthur has with the Goddess through her embodiment as Queen Guinevere. The search for the Holy Grail really was a search for the womb of the Goddess, the cup of healing and compassion to restore the relationship and restore the people, king, and land.

Those who walk the king's path can have difficult relationships, for the call to service always will come first over mortal loves and family, unless that identity of service is built into family structure and duty. Those on this path are drawn to family and socialization, enjoying the fruits and blessings of the path. Those on the king's path are selfless, often to the point of destructiveness, sacrificing the self unnecessarily at times. Now, at the end of our Piscean Age, many people find this path attractive, identifying with the role of the martyr as sacrificed king, but the death and rebirth need not be physical or even emotional. The service can be executed ritually, through walking the Wheel of the Year and mediating the powers at every spoke and every turn. There the king is born, dies, and is reborn, and the Earth is renewed through the celebration with community, yet no one needs to sacrifice the entirety of their life's blood or destroy their life.

Priests of the Wheel of the Year

The sacred kings really are priest-kings, ministers who connect the people with the land, with the depths, and with the stars. The combination of spiritual and terrestrial rulership has been lost on most cultures, but is seen clearly in the mysticism of the East and in ancient Egypt, and only echoed in shadow in our Arthurian myth cycle. Such rulers were deified in life and in death, as mediators of powerful forces, connecting the living people with the gods and powers of creation.

Today, many modern pagans seek to emulate the ways of celebration. The Wheel of the Year, combining the Celtic fire festivals with the solar holidays of solstice and equinox, attune and harmonize the Witch with the cycles and seasons, yet usually do not fulfill the sacred duty of the king's path: turning the wheel through an exchange of energy, a sacrifice, between the worlds (chart 14).

Holiday	Energetic Movement
Samhain	All gates open and energy passes freely. Upper World and Middle World energies tend to descend to the Lower World, while Lower World energy rises to the Middle World.
Yule	Energy moves from the Lower World to the Upper World with the rebirth of the Sun Child through the darkness.
Imbolc	Energy moves from the Upper World to the Lower World to awaken the Goddess from her slumber and quicken the land.
Ostara	Energy moves from the Lower World to the Middle World with the rising of the Goddess as the Lady of Flowers.
Beltane	All gates open and energy tends to focus on the Middle World.
Litha	Energy moves from the Upper World to the Middle World as the power of the Sun God merges with that of the Goddess of the Land.
Lammas	Energy moves from the Middle World to the Upper World as the Grain God is sacrificed and life force is released.
Mabon	Energy moves from the Middle World to the Lower World as the Sacrificed God's spirit descends.

CHART 14: ENERGETIC FLOW OF THE WHEEL OF THE YEAR

The Wheel of the Year is but one loom among humanity, who are like cogs within the machinery of the universe, all spinning the threads and forming the tapestry of the weaver goddess. Near our Wheel of Fate, of cycles and seasons in the Middle World, there is the Wheel of Justice in the Underworld, the realm where many seemingly retributive powers rise, and the Wheel of Judgment, of aeons and cosmic cycles, in the heavenly world (figure 17). The three interlock, and the turning of the wheels is what keeps creation spinning. The three wheels in this form are taught explicitly in the Merlin tarot work of R. J. Stewart, but can be seen in mythology and adapted by modern magicians. Each seasonal holiday focuses the built-up power from one realm onto another, facilitating the turning of the wheels. Each of the three realms has its own administrators, priest-kings, in the worlds of humans, fey, and angels. All three races are necessary for the functioning of the universe.

In the next seasonal celebration you experience, take the role of the priest-king. Walk the dragon's path and make an offering of energy at the ritual. Sacrifice the Cone of Power in your circle to turn the Wheel of the Year, rather than manifest

FIGURE 17: THREE WHEELS OF THE THREE WORLDS

spells for personal gain. Use this ritual to harmonize with the Earth, Sun and cosmos, partnering with the priestesses and priests on the other side of the veil in the Great Above, Great Below, and Great Between.

Through communion with the divine in service, right relationships can be restored among people, the land, and the heavens. Divine will can be sovereign. Many people intuitively take the role of the priest-king in leadership positions in secular roles, yet still confer a bit of the mysteries. Our ancient hunter and warrior mysteries, which ultimately revolve around bringing back food for the tribe, form the core of this mystery, and both ancient and modern forms of hunting, warrior skills, martial arts, and leadership can lead to this road. What our world needs now is for more people to formally mediate the energy of the king's death and rebirth as priests for the greater community, forging new ways out of the old.

The Faery Path

The road of the second ray is the road of the faery path. Like the king's path, it, too, is associated with the land and energy lines. The tracks connecting sacred sites were called faery tracks or ghost roads. Sometimes they were straight tracks, like the dragon lines. Others were curved waves spiraling out of the vortex of Earth energy where the faeries were said to gather and dance in secret. The faery path is difficult to choose. You simply must be called to it and accept the calling. It is for those who are faery touched. Perhaps they have been of the blood of the bright and shining ones, so it is running through their veins and is awakened. Perhaps they have walked the other paths in previous lives, as it is said that this path indicates the untangling of the threads of fate, the wyrd or karma of past actions. Often those who are faery touched are atoning for something, or taking actions now that they will atone for in a future life. These people can be primal in temperament, seeming more like a force of nature walking in the form of a woman or man rather than a human wielding the forces of nature. They simply seem to be in harmony with these forces, with their moods and thoughts reflected in the environment and weather.

In any case, those on the faery path have great natural ability, in particular the gifts of sight and feeling. Sometimes the gifts are so strong that they are overwhelming. Some are even born with the sign of the caul, the birth sack veiling their face when born, the sign of a seer. This is a key sign that one with sight, one who might be faery touched, has been born, able to see beyond the veil, into the past, present, and future, to commune with the spirits of the dead and the fey. Those on the faery path know what to do in life and in magick, but they do not know why they know. Nature itself seems to speak to them in omens and portents, signs and symbols, and they speak back to nature. Their relationships with the plants, animals, and elemental world come naturally.

Just as the king's path is one of the warrior, so is the faery path one of the adventurer. Those who are touched by the fey, who feel in between, usually find they don't fit in with most groups and organizations, unless they forge their own group. They wander, following the omens of nature and their own whims, until a new course of action is evident. Everything is new and exciting, and they have a childlike innocence and wonder.

The key to this path is kinship with the faery allies. One must be able to consciously have communion with the fey to fully evolve on this path. There is a sense of being "between" the worlds of flesh and blood and the worlds of Elfland. This sense of betweenness, dual perspective, grants tremendous insight. One can approach the truth from two sides rather than just the limited human perspective. To be able to see with both eyes of flesh and eyes of light is quite a remarkable gift and a heavy responsibility.

Faery Offerings

One of the traditional "keys" to opening good relations with Elphame and the Good Folk is to make offerings to them. Offerings create a spiritual bridge between the lands, opening the way of mutual communication and blessing. As with the king's path, where energy is exchanged through sacrifice, literal or ritual, faery offerings are like small sacrifices. They appear as beacons to the spirit world, and sustain the relationship once established.

Faery offerings are best made someplace outside. A special altar in nature can be made. I prefer a flat garden stone reserved for my offerings. Indoor offerings and altars should be reserved for the offerings to the home spirit or house elf, not to the realm of faery in general. The best offerings are items that have been worked on or collected by human hands and cannot occur in nature. They require our effort, and sharing them with the fey is a "sacrifice" of our effort, our time and energy. Traditional offerings include bread, honey, milk, butter, pastries, beer, wine, and hard alcohol. In the Americas, traditional offerings include tobacco, cornmeal, chocolate, and cocoa leaves, depending on the tradition and locale.

Make your offerings heartfelt. Bless the offering with your intention and energy. Call out to the faery realm and say:

> *In the name of the Lady and Lord, by the three powers, I offer this*
> *to you in love and trust. May there always be peace between us.*
> *Blessed be.*

Offerings should be left out only for a day or so, then either buried, if possible, or disposed of in a respectful way. Liquids can be poured on the land if not done so as part of the offering ritual. The "energy" of the offering is consumed by the spirits. Animals that consume it are doing so as emissaries of the spirits, but people should not consume offerings to the spirits and faery. This is considered bad manners and, with the life force removed from the food, can make humans sick.

One drawback of the faery path is that those on it not only have difficulty relating to "normal" people but also can feel as if they have descended into madness, in Faerie, where the normal rules of reality do not make sense. Time and space can seem distorted. One is quite literally touched, by blood or spirit, in all senses of the word. The touch can bring wisdom, but it also can take more than it gives. Many people who are not on the path but are touched by the fey, who haven't heard the call and learned the necessary coping skills, descend quite easily into madness. It can take quite an effort to ground oneself and return the faery wisdom and insight to the land of flesh and blood.

The Cunning Path

The way of the third ray, the crooked road, is the cunning path of Witchcraft. It is a path that takes elements from the other two paths, serpenting back and forth between them, yet finds its own way. One on this path slips between the service of the king's way, yet the service is not always so grand and formal. Most often the service is one-on-one, offering a bit of advice, a potion, or a look at the cards. In days past, it sometimes would be the grand rituals of the priestess and priest of the temples, but it also was the path of the simple ways of the farm and crossroads, to bless the fields and animals.

On the other hand, those on the cunning path also must stand between, like those on the faery path. Perhaps this betweenness is not a constant state of being for the Cunning Ones. They stand not simultaneously in both worlds but at the edge of each, with one foot in and one foot out of each realm. They stand on the edge of civilization, the edge of cultivated and wild and the edge of nature and super nature. They can step into either world and just as easily step back out again. They can speak for the spirits, and are extended kin to the spirits, but they are not as surrounded by the spirits as are those who are faery touched. Those on the cunning path often are not touched at all, and have to work hard for every bit of power, every scrap of knowledge. They watch and observe. They listen and write. They speak to teachers of flesh and spirit, remembering their previous lives and gathering their wisdom, sometimes at a great price.

There are no rules that bind people on this path, except those they create for themselves. There is no need for sacrifice, unless they so choose. There is no need for madness, unless they choose. Yet they might choose either or both if necessary.

While the warriors are found on the king's path and the adventurers are on the faery path, the Wise Woman and Wise Man are found on the cunning path. Though they may venture for a time and fight when necessary, there is a "root-edness" to their home and to their people, yet a separation from them as well. They are wyrd, and live on the edge, even when beloved and welcomed. They do not fear the dark, and they take that which doesn't serve and transform it, so it can serve again, like rotting vegetables that are turned into rich soil compost. Everything serves. Everything returns. Everything feeds everything else. They help this process along, for there is wisdom in this way.

Those on the cunning path are called upon by others to turn the Wheel, sometimes the Wheel as it spins as the Year and other times the Wheels of Fate, Justice, and Judgment. Their Witch's soul moves the Wheel for themselves and for others. They become agents of fate and time, aspiring to be keepers of the Timeless Tradition of the Nameless Art.

The Witch's Walk

The simple act of walking is an act of magick and Witchcraft. Witchcraft is a journey, and moving from normal civilization to the edge of human conscious-ness and back again is a powerful ritual. Some do it through visionary work and ritual, and some experience it through literally walking from their home to the wilds of nature. Each step is an opportunity for both inner contemplation and outer awareness. We feel the rhythm of our bodies moving at a pace and know that everything has its pace. Everything has its rhythms, cycles, and seasons. That rhythm becomes a constant backdrop to induce the relaxed cycles of trance, opening our perceptions to deeper thought, inspiration, and psychic sight.

Yet each step is a movement in flesh and blood. Each step can bring a great awareness of our flesh, such as how it feels in a shoe upon the Earth. We feel our breath more acutely, as well as the temperature of the air entering our body. We feel our vigor and strength and become more aware of our weaknesses, pains, and joints. We feel the cycles ebb and flow in the world of flesh and form.

While still walking and retaining an awareness of our bodily senses, we also receive information from the spirit world. When we do, the sights and smells of the world become clearer. We feel temperature and hear the noises of humanity and nature. We also can seek out the voices of nature, of the goddesses and gods of our land, by looking for omens and seeking meaning in what we see and hear when we ask questions of our gods.

Ask a question you have of your life, something for which you need divine guidance. It can be a question about the past, present, or future, or about what you should do in a specific situation. Ask your question as clearly as possible. Ask the spirit and gods of the land who have your highest and best interests at heart to answer the question for your own good, harming none.

Then begin your walk in nature. Walk to a threshold point, someplace that is between. Crossroads, cemeteries, swamps, hedges, the boundary between forest and field, or a shoreline all are great places that are liminal and represent a threshold. Doorways, archways, or the line between city and suburb also can be threshold points. Then turn around clockwise three times with your eyes closed. Open them and look around. What do you see? Look from left to right, but also up, down, and right before you. Does anything you see, hear, smell, or feel answer your question? Traditionally the movement of animals and the locations of plants and trees were omens, but today we can include cars and trucks, planes, and pedestrians. Let your intuition guide you, and see and feel what truly is there rather than what you think the answer should be.

This walking divination can be enhanced by being "between" before you begin the journey, and explains some "markings" that traditionally indicate a Witch. Wearing two different colored socks, or one sock inside-out, puts you between. Wearing other clothing inside-out, such as a shirt, is another method. Half-shaving, half-dressing, wearing two different shoes, and even half-eating a meal right before you begin are methods of inducing this state of between consciousness, and the restoration of "normal" clothing or completing the meal or other action are good ways to return to a more traditional awareness.

While taking a magickal walk is an escape to another reality through shifting our consciousness, it also is an opportunity to feel the body and world, to truly commune with it. In essence, this is what both magick and meditation are for the Witch. We must bilocate, hold two positions (if not more than two) in space and time at once, and shift in and out while remaining functional for ourselves, for our people and the world. Walking, quite literally between the worlds, hones our skills so we then can be of service to the world.

The Blood

The path of the mysteries changes those who truly walk it. It changes us spiritually, but before we can realize those changes there must be transformations in our mind, our emotions, and our body. Sometimes the changes are subtle, and sometimes they are profound. One of the ways these changes are described is to say the blood is changed. This might appear to be a metaphor, but to many of us on the path it is not just a poetic metaphor but can be quite literal. We believe the power of initiation, the power of ritual, can awaken not only forces within us, energetically within our soul, but also the gifts and memories of our ancestors, genetic memory encoded in our DNA, in our blood.

British Traditional Wicca lineages such as the Gardnerians and Alexandrians have a blessing that seems very Crowley influenced, usually done in third-degree initiation rituals where by the gods' power they call for the light to "crystallize in our blood, fulfilling us of resurrection, for there is no part of us that is not of the gods." The light crystallizes in the blood, ideally with this divine power, for the resurrection mysteries of initiation. The blood itself—consisting of water, blood cells containing our DNA, minerals, and metals such as iron—acts metaphysically like a crystal. In magick and healing, crystals are "programmed" with your intention to bring out certain inherent qualities found within the mineral. You can carry a stone around for healing, but it is much more effective if the crystal has been consecrated, hallowed through the psychic light of your intention, to awaken its natural power. Then it will be effective. It seems as if a similar effect, on a more profound personal level, is taking place here. In crystal healing work, some teachers look at the water and blood of the body, along with the DNA molecules, the minerals, metals, and vitamins, as being similar to crystalline structure, one that can be programmed for healing and power.

Blood is a powerful aspect of magick. Though many Witches don't like to talk about it and, in fact, don't learn about it in an effort to be more socially accepted, blood has played a role in traditional pagan magick. Blood in many cultures is the medium that contains our life force and, in our case, our Witch power. The circulatory system is one part of our body that helps keep the life force flowing, along with our nervous system and energy meridians. Each flows with a different aspect of life force. But the blood is just as important. In some traditions of the Craft, a Witch is not made, but born. One must be "of the blood," of a family line that contains and passes the power. Those Witches who are initiated are said to be of the blood already, having a genetic connection to Witchcraft. Most people are not raised in an environment where such natural talents are encouraged. Initiation rituals are designed to welcome someone with such a predisposition back into the fold and encourage the development of their Craft abilities. Author Orion Foxwood described an initiation blessing where the initiator says, "I touch you and your blood remembers!" One's blood is awakened to the memories, but such memories can be awakened only if the Witchblood is inherently there, waiting.

This teaching can seem rather racist to the outside observer. We live in a time and place where anybody can be almost anything if they work hard enough. Shouldn't Witchcraft be the same? They say a Witch can be made, not born, but at a great price, and it requires an effort much greater than simply reading a few books on magick. Controversial Witch Robert Cochrane said: "A Witch is born, and not made; or if one is to be made, then tears must be spilt before the moon can be drawn. For the Lady chooses whom she will to be Her Lover, and She loves the most She rends apart before making them Wise."

Less conservative teachers will say that ultimately we all are of the blood. We all have some form of pagan ancestry and pagan magick within us, and training, rituals, vision, and initiation can awaken that pagan magick within us. Our blood calls out to the ancestors and seeks to walk the path again.

In my practice of the three rays work, I've found that the rituals of visionary initiation do indeed change the blood. They rebuild you in a fundamental way, from the DNA to the three souls and beyond. It has been described as a transformation, a shifting of color and awareness. That is not to say that, if we were physically cut, our blood would be a different color, yet it is more than poetic inference. I believe the colors reflect a fundamental change in our light and life force, and circulate through the many layers of the aura, influencing the way people and spirits perceive us.

We all start this journey, in this body, with the red blood of the living creatures. We embody the third ray as one of the races of flesh and blood, and like most creatures of flesh and blood, our blood runs red. We do have the opportunity to unite with other intelligences and our own divine essence, and become more than human, going beyond the limited perspective of humanity, holding the consciousness of both nature and super nature. As we do, our blood reflects the transformation occurring within us into something "other." We awaken that which is already there, or forge something new and different, crafting both soul and body into wondrous levels of transhuman consciousness.

Those who are walking the straight path of kings transform their blood much as the alchemical ladder turns lead into gold. The blood is associated primarily with iron, and iron represents the third rung on the alchemical ladder, with lead and tin below it and copper, quicksilver, silver, and gold above it. Like the warrior holding the iron-forged sword, there is a transformation from warrior to chieftain, from the iron through the other metals and eventually to gold, like the gold of the king's crown. The blood turns to gold within those on the king's path, reflecting the light of the stars. The gold leads to the forging of the king's sovereignty, connecting the light of the heavens, through the flesh, to the metals of the Earth.

Those who are faery touched have the potential to transform the blood at least twice. Once they change the blood from red to green—for they have been touched with the blessing of nature, often through an ordeal—there is opportunity for a second transformation to the blue blood of faery. The ordeal of nature leads them to replace their blood, really their life force, with the sap of the plant world, with the medicine of their tree teachers and plant allies, the balms and banes of the Witch's garden. Their blood flows like sap, thick and green, and they become attuned to the realm of nature. This blessing can grant them a deeper knowledge and communion with the plant world, the power of healing, and awaken their faery nature on an even deeper level.

Those who are called by faery hands to an ordeal in the Underworld can find themselves replacing red or green blood with the enchanted blue fire of Elphame. The depths run bright with fountains and rivers of blue faery flame. Many of us learn to call it up as blue fire to cast our circles and set our wards. The blue fire is found in the heart of the Earth and in the courts of the Queen and King of Fey. To have your blood flow blue is to attune to the nature of the archfey, the Sidhe beneath the hills. It signifies a union with them, a partnership, brotherhood, or lover connection to one or more. It is an adoption into their tribe and a sharing of their love and powerful nature.

Those who are called to the crooked path have no clear-cut step. We are creatures of the red blood, and in many ways we remain creatures of the red blood. Yet we synthesize aspects of both of the other paths. Rather than find ourselves going though the ladder of alchemy, reflecting the heavens on the Earth, we descend through the gates of initiation. Like the Goddess of old legends and the Witchcraft initiation rituals past and present, we face the guardian at the threshold of each level of Underworld, seven in all, and have to renounce something that makes us who and what we are (chart 15). We become unmade, one step at a time, and with each step of unmaking we free the energy of our consciousness to do new and wonderful things. By letting go of facets of the self that hold identity, we also let go of facets of the self that hold limitations. By releasing those limitations, we become free. The descent of the Goddess is the model of initiation on the crooked path, particularly in the tale of Inanna, Queen of Heaven and Earth, but in many ways the descent within our body, mirrored in both the heavens and the Earth, is the key teaching. We find a model of the chakras to be a helpful map to understand the inner descent and rise. We descend from the head through the gates to the heart and downward to the base of our spine. Then we rise again, reforging ourselves anew and choosing who and what we become.

Gate	Item Relinquished by the Goddess	Chakra
First gate	Crown	Crown
Second gate	Single-stranded necklace	Brow
Third gate	Double-stranded necklace	Throat
Fourth gate	Breastplate	Heart
Fifth gate	Gold ring or bracelet	Solar plexus
Sixth gate	Measuring line and rod	Belly
Seventh gate	Robe	Root

CHART 15: SEVEN GATES OF THE GODDESS

Rather than find ourselves flowing with sap or fire from another world and another race, we reforge our race, creating our own Witch self. We see ourselves as "other" sitting on the edge, liminal, unseen. It is our own self we find or forge, and with whom we switch blood. Does our blood stay red? Yes, in many ways. Does it glow with the golden yellow wisdom of the third ray? Yes, particularly when we are curving toward the teaching of will and power. Does it glow green and blue with nature's touch? Yes, particularly when we lean toward the faery ray of love and trust. Do the colors come together in a vibrant amalgam of red and blue, turning the bright violet of alchemists and magicians, flecked with gold and silver and emerald? Yes! Our blood burns with the violet flame of magick, opalescent, reflecting all that is, was, and ever shall be.

Sovereignty

The transformation of the blood along the three paths leads to the paths of royalty. All become blessed as royals, not just the kings and warriors. The blood is consecrated and becomes the royal blood of the heavens, Earth, and Underworld.

Sovereignty is the name of the ancient Goddess of the Land. It is she whom we serve when walking the Middle World's ways, enfleshed. We each find her wisdom, become her consort, male or female it matters not. Each path leads us to a different kind of rule. Each path forges a different crown.

Those on the king's path forge crowns by entering into a relationship with the land. Though they walk the path most strongly associated with the heavens, they bring the stellar and solar light of the heavens down and manifest it in the material world. They find union with the Goddess of the Earth. Warrior queens on the path find union with the Green Man, the green flesh upon the Earth. The sovereignty of the king or queen is based on the honorable relationship with the land. If integrity with the land is lost, then so is their Crown of Humility and enlightenment. Many who follow this path successfully are interred in the land as our Sleepers, the secret kings and queens whose bodies have been preserved, mummified beneath the land. Their consciousness remains with them, and they have volunteered for this service, to mediate the energies of the past and future and the energies between humanity and the land where they are buried. They are record keepers and preservers of our community during the coming changes. As more of their slumbers are disturbed, there are fewer and fewer of these ancient ones to carry on the task, and soon more will be needed.

Those on the faery path find symbiosis with a faery union. They walk the path most strongly associated with the land and with the depths, and they must bring the life up from the depths through their contact with the elder race. First these potential initiates find that their adventuring leads to an encounter and eventual relationship with their Co-Walker or Double, who often later turns into a faery lover The love is magickally consummated, and through that love, gnosis, direct spirit knowledge, is experienced. Those who find a mate among the Ladies and Lords of Elfland can develop the relationship further with a faery marriage, a permanent union with a Faery King or Faery Queen. Bonded, two become one. A bit of you will now reside forever in the other realms of Faerie with your love, but likewise a bit of your bride or husband always will reside with you. A permanent bridge between humanity and the elder race is developed, lasting until your death. Then you may choose to return to the realm of your consort for eternity, draw in with those elders of our Mighty Dead, or spin the wheel and walk the world again.

Those on the cunning path find enlightenment through the self, while still honoring the land, the stars, and the deep. Their path is involutionary, and they forge their crown out of their own experiences, their own gathered wisdom, love, and power. Like Odin or Othin hanging from the World Tree Yggdrasil, offering "myself to myself," those of us on the cunning path remember that we were the first Witch, the first sorcerer, and we will be the last Witch, and we all have been Witches in between, in an infinite chain stretching forward and backward through time. We then come into our own sovereignty, forged through our own work, as we have made ourselves, undone and unraveled ourselves seeking the mystery, and rebirthed ourselves into whom and what we desire to be. We become Witch Queens and Witch Kings alike in power, regardless of coven, rank, or title. Only those who wear the crown truly recognize others who do as well. Upon the conclusion of our journey, our three selves speak as one with the Crown of Humility, and we join our elders among the Hidden Company, if we so choose, for in essence we never left. We always have been there, guiding ourselves, waiting for ourselves to return.

Keep in mind the lessons of King Arthur and Merlin, of Guinevere and Morgan, be they fiction or fact. Just because one attains spiritual mastery doesn't mean one cannot lose it again. At certain points on all the paths, the crown can become tarnished. The crown can be knocked from our heads. We can fall out of mastery and relationship with our path. The only course of action after such events is to redeem ourselves and walk the path again, truer than before.

Each of the paths opens not only a path of initiation but also a potential path for ascension, for enlightenment, to reach a new level of consciousness beyond the ordinary human realm. Yet each path has its own traps and pitfalls.

To ascend through the king's path of will, you become "more" of whatever you are. It amplifies whatever nature you possess. This is the journey of some magicians, to become Ipsissimus, the "utmost self" at the top of the Tree. Yet those on a path of power also can magnify unwanted traits. An unchecked ego will grow. Hunger for power simply for the sake of power, for control, can grow on this path.

Ascension through the faery path, through love, expands the energy body. Our consciousness simply expands with more love, to include all of nature. Yet those who do not understand Perfect Love may become lost in sentiment and romance, losing sight of the true blessings of love and nature for what is perceived as a human ideal. Such people usually end up delusional or disenchanted, in all senses of the word.

To ascend through wisdom on the crooked path involves both love and will. Wisdom will focus your will and expand it to fill the energy body of your consciousness. This is perhaps the most balanced path of the three, yet one can get caught in the quest for knowledge, in facts, figures, and obscure and arcane minutiae, losing sight of the true goal on the path of wisdom, of the Witch. In Qabalah, it is the trap of Da'ath, where otherwise good magicians lose themselves on the quest.

The three rays each contain a gate of initiation. Each of the paths offers an opportunity to transform our consciousness into something greater, connecting with the teachings of the path and the spirits of the Otherworld to forge a new future. While we can hope to choose the path that best suits our temperament, sometimes one path calls to us more than another on a soul level, disregarding the choices our personality would make and leading us to the gate that will best serve us on the path to evolution.

The Winding Way

The Winding Way,
The Crooked Road,
The Old Straight Track,
Where do they go?
Wax and wither,
To and fro.
The Path of the Wise,
The Road of the Night.
The Emerald Heart,
The Torch of Light.
The Lightning Strikes,
Thunder Bright.
The Faery Queen,
The Mighty Dead,
The Angelic Might,
Give Fire in the Head.
Flesh and Blood,
Green, Gold, and Red.

CHAPTER NINE: THE GARDEN OF THE GODS

And the LORD God said, Behold, the man is become as one of us, to know good and evil: and now, lest he put forth his hand, and take also of the tree of life, and eat, and live for ever: Therefore the LORD God sent him forth from the garden of Eden, to till the ground from whence he was taken. So he drove out the man; and he placed at the east of the garden of Eden Cherubims, and a flaming sword which turned every way, to keep the way of the tree of life. —Genesis 3:20–24

The Garden of the Gods is the name of both a ritual I devised several years ago and a state of consciousness that the ritual aims to achieve. It represents the first work I did with the three rays of Witchcraft, using them as invocations of primary powers and calling them to the ritual space much the way others would call upon deities and spirits. The experiences were profound not only for me but also for others when I began sharing the technique publicly. They have become a major adaptation to my own personal private work and my work with the public.

The Garden of the Gods refers to the primeval vision of the Earth, the True Garden of Union. Many mythologies have a concept of a "fall," a loss of innocence and a punishment, being cast out from the Garden. We see it in the legends of Shamballa, Tara, Avalon, Hesperides, Atlantis, and Lemuria. We see it most of all in the Judeo-Christian legend of Eden. One of the important things to understand in paganism is that we have no true fall mythos. We have rebellious gods like Prometheus stealing fire, or more Gnostic tales of descent to bring forth life into the world, but we have no concept of sin and personal punishment. We have only the balance of Adjustment, the term Crowley used in his Thoth Tarot for the card that was once called Justice. Be it karma or wyrd, it is not personal, but is simply the result of what has happened before.

Our fall really is an allegory for moving from our simpler hunter-gatherer societies, to agrarian lifestyles, and eventually to our "civilized" forms of buildings, writing, and commerce. Each step took us away from a natural, more animal-like lifestyle, dependent on what the earth had to offer, rather than staying stationary, settling the earth, and working it. This separation allowed us to enter into a different relationship with plants, animals, minerals, and ultimately the Earth itself.

Though our evolution can seem destructive, and it is, it mimics the separation of alchemy. In alchemy, the motto is to "dissolve and coagulate." Things are continuously dissolved, separated, and rejoined, to attain a higher state of purity and refinement. Our particular historical epoch happens to be occurring at the end of a separation and possibly at the start of a new rejoining. Separation is a necessary step for the evolution and advancement of the whole.

In Qabalistic lore, this separation is described as the creation of Da'ath, the false sephira that is the hole within the Tree of Life, separating the bottom seven spheres from the top three. Originally, Malkuth, the World, was closest to the higher spheres of Goddess, God, and Great Spirit. But it contained the entire potential of the Tree, like seeds within a fruit. The fruit "fell" from the Tree, landing at the bottom, in the material world, and this is the source of all our other stories of the "fall" from divine grace. Yet all fruit needs to fall so new trees can be born. As we grow up toward the light, toward the source, not only are we redeemed and restored, but our evolution makes all of creation richer for our experiences. Our mythologies make this climb hard, as Da'ath, or Knowledge, is described as the opening to the Abyss, the land of demons. But only by facing what separates us can we find union again.

A modern pagan mythos, as taught by pagan elder Oberon Zell, gives us a possible explanation about our relationship to the people of Eden. We are the "other people" that show up later in the story, giving us a mythical connection to our personal sense of "otherness." Biblical mythos has come to dominate our culture, even in a land that purports to have a separation of Church and State. We all are more familiar with the biblical myth than the Norse, Celtic, or Meso-American ones. It's become a part of our cultural context. So how do modern pagans fit into that mythos? We were the Other People, east of Eden. Though we often believe the story that Adam and Eve were the first humans, they were simply the first people in Eden. Eventually, their murderous child Cain left and found shelter with the people in the Land of Nod, east of Eden, and took a wife. Who were those people? Where did they come from? They were children of the other gods, not the god of Eden. These people had no original sin. They were never cast out of the creation, the garden of their god. We are their spiritual descendants, yet we live in a society in which we all have bought into the "fall" mythos. We need only remember that we never left our garden, and the magickal nature of the world springs up around us.

This magickal state of union with nature, with stone, plant, and animal, with each other and with the spirits, gods, and angels, is the Garden of the Gods. It's a renewed consciousness, not simply returning to that primal state but returning to that state with the knowledge we gained while we believed we were outside that state. We come back with greater appreciation of the garden and our union with the gods. We return like serpents, wiser for our experience. And that is the essence of uniting our love and power to find this wisdom. If everyone and everything were already perfect, then we would not appreciate their perfection. Only through our sense of separation from divine perfection and the free will to consciously choose love and power simultaneously do we find true wisdom.

The Garden of the Gods ritual itself takes place in what I call the Grand Circle. Most Witches do their work in a magick circle, a ritual space acknowledging the four directions and the four elemental powers associated with it, between the worlds. In this between state, we touch all worlds and can better work our otherworldly ways. The Grand Circle is not simply a bubble between the worlds, but is a circle cast in the Middle World, Lower World, and Underworld, each with its own set of four directional guardians, making twelve "quarters" in total.

The guardians of the Middle World are animal spirits, and the elements are arranged in the seasonal orientation familiar to most Wiccans and ceremonial magicians (chart 16).

Direction	Element	Season	Animal Spirit
North	Earth	Winter	Snake
East	Air	Spring	Bat
South	Fire	Summer	Wolf
West	Water	Autumn	Frog

CHART 16: CIRCLE OF THE MIDDLE WORLD

The guardians of the Underworld are plant totems, though they could just as easily be faery allies. They are arranged in accord with the alchemical mandala of transformation, similar to the structure formed in the work of the Greek philosopher Empedocles (chart 17).

Direction	Element	Alchemical Quality	Plant
North	Earth	Cold and dry	Mandrake
East	Fire	Warm and dry	Monkshood
South	Air	Warm and moist	Henbane
West	Water	Cold and moist	Datura

CHART 17: CIRCLE OF THE UNDERWORLD

Lastly, the Upper World elements are arranged according to the patterns of the fixed signs of the zodiac, as well as the various fixed stars associated with the directions, giving us the most unusual elemental arrangement yet (chart 18). The four traditional archangels are associated with the signs and directions in this circle.

Direction	Element	Sign	Star	Angel
North	Air	Aquarius	Fomalhaut	Raphael
East	Earth	Taurus	Aldebaran	Uriel
South	Fire	Leo	Regulus	Michael
West	Water	Scorpio	Antares	Gabriel

CHART 18: CIRCLE OF THE UPPER WORLD

All together, the twelve gates in the three worlds can have further zodiac correspondences that are only implied and not stated outright in the ritual. The signs of the Middle World are aligned with the mutable signs (Gemini, Virgo, Sagittarius, Pisces), for the Middle World is the place of change. The signs of the Underworld are aligned with the cardinal signs (Aries, Cancer, Libra, Capricorn), for the Underworld is the place of initiation and confrontation. This gives us some interesting correspondences and techniques when we want to do a "simple" circle specifically aligned with any of the three worlds individually.

The "circle" first takes form as a pillar of light from the Lower, Middle, and Upper Worlds, but in reality it is like an infinity loop, as the stars of the heavens lead to the darkness of the Underworld and the darkness leads to the stars, and one feeds into the other (figure 18). We stand not just between the worlds, but in infinity, where all is one, yet there is a multitude of expressions of that one within the garden. It is the ouroboros serpent that eats its own tail. The end leads to its beginning again.

FIGURE 18: INFINITY SYMBOL

The Grand Circle of the Garden of the Gods is best practiced by a small, dedicated group or a capable individual. All members should be thoroughly familiar with more traditional circle magick techniques before attempting this working.

The original version of this Grand Circle, first done publicly for a Samhain rite, features more traditionally "dark" spirit guardians, particularly those animal and baneful plant spirits with strong associations with European Witchcraft. You can alter the chosen guardians to suit the season, your own spiritual connections, and the personal preferences of the group performing the ritual.

The Great Spirit

The three rays emanate from a central source, the creative principle of the universe. Communion with this source is central to the level of consciousness we experience as the Garden of the Gods. Many modern teachings say that in the next aeon we are to create Heaven on Earth, and to do so we must understand the source, for Heaven on Earth is simply living in constant communion with the source.

Many Witchcraft traditions can be considered dualistic, looking at the divine as an interplay between two primary forces. Many of us are familiar with the Taoist symbols and terminology of yin-yang, a divided circle of black and white, each with a small seed of the other within it. Light contains dark, and dark contains light. In the Northern traditions of European paganism, the interplay occurs between fire and ice, resulting in the creation of the universe. In Wicca and many other Witchcraft traditions, these primal forces are alive and conscious and seen as the Great Goddess and Great God. Together they move as one to create the universe we know. Together they are the central source of creation and destruction.

In Hermetic lore, the source of creation is known as the Divine Mind. In the Hermetic document known as *The Kybalion*, this wisdom is summed up in the Principle of Mentalism: "Everything is a thought within the Divine Mind."

Everything seen and unseen is a thought within the Divine Mind. The nature of the universe is mental. It is a creative expression of the source through the process of divine thought.

While at heart I'm a Hermetic Witch, and I agree wholeheartedly with the Principle of Mentalism, after many experiences, visions, and intuitions, I think this principle is only part of the picture, only part of our understanding of the divine. Many traditions teach that humanity is made in the image of the divine. We share a nature with the divine. A Hermeticist would say that because the divine has a mental nature, and we have a mind, a mental nature, and the divine creates, we too can create. This creative thought power is what bonds us. It is how we are like the divine.

Still, I believe we fundamentally are triune beings, so therefore would not the nature of the divine be triune? While the magician places the emphasis of the divine on the mind, does not the divine also have will? Magicians often talk about divine will, that the magician's or mystic's will is simply an expression of the divine's will. Magick is the process of aligning your own personal will with the will of the higher self, and therefore the will of the divine.

Does the divine also have love? So many religions focus on the essence of the divine being love. Divine love is not a personal love, an unconditional, all-pervading mystical love. Witches call that Perfect Love. Christians might call it the sacred heart of Christ. Modern mystics tend to call it Christ consciousness, the consciousness of unconditional love. In Qabalistic lore, this level of consciousness is expressed in the middle triangle of the Tree of Life, notably in the central sphere of Tiphereth, and the sphere of Chesed, of Mercy, of the highest level of unconditional love we can understand while being incarnated in the body.

Magickal traditions try to name the divine, beyond manifestations of the Goddess and God, and to find words that express the all-encompassing nature of the divine, yet they often focus on only one of the three aspects of the divine. Different traditions relate to the divine through their own lens. Each tradition could be said to focus on one of the three rays, one of the pillars, in seeking out the divine, which clouds their perception of the whole.

In my own mystical experiences, the best way I relate to the ineffable is to do the unthinkable and to divide the indivisible. By looking at the divine through three lenses, we might not see it completely, but we get a larger perspective of the whole (chart 19). To me, the divine is not only the Divine Mind, but also a triquetra linking the Divine Mind to a Divine Heart and a Divine Will (figure 19).

FIGURE 19: DIVINE TRIQUETRA

Divinity	Ray	Name	Description
Divine Will	First ray	Dryghten	Lord, Ancient Providence, unifying essence, "original source of all things all-knowing, all-pervading, all-powerful; changeless, eternal"
Divine Heart	Second ray	CeliCed	Celi—Hidden god of heaven and source before the Sun was revealed, Ced—Hidden feminine power within the Earth that unites with Celi
Divine Mind	Third ray	Cruithear	Creator, shaper, giver of form

CHART 19: TRIUNE DIVINITY

In my own practice, I use the term Great Spirit to denote the divine creative force, beyond the Goddess and God. It is triune with the Goddess and God, but on its own I believe it is triune in nature, encompassing the Divine Mind, Heart, and Will. By looking at other traditions, particularly pagan ones, and their terms for the divine, we can gather greater understanding of our ancestors and flesh out our own understanding of the three rays expressed through the divine.

In Gardnerian Wicca, the term Dryghten is used to denote the Great Spirit. Dryghten is a term usually translated as "Lord." In some Old English Bibles,

Dryghten is the term used for JHVH, or Jehovah. Garnderians see it as a nongender-specific form of "Lord" used to denote a divine creative source. Some interpret it as a divinity that is all-encompassing and panentheistic. Others interpret it as being more akin to a divinity such as that found in the African diasporic traditions of Vodou, where this "Lord" is distant and separate from creation, with the Goddess and God as the personal and intermediary entities guiding creation. The "Dryghten Blessing Prayer" can be found in some branches of the Gardnerian Book of Shadows, and was revealed to the public by Patricia Crowther in her book *The Diary of a Witch High Priestess*.

> *In the name of Dryghten, the Ancient Providence,*
> *Who was from the beginning and is for eternity,*
> *Male and Female, the Original Source of all things;*
> *all-knowing, all-pervading, all-powerful;*
> *changeless, eternal.*

> *In the name of the Lady of the Moon,*
> *and the Lord of Death and Resurrection.*

> *In the name of the Mighty Ones of the Four Quarters,*
> *the Kings of the Elements.*

> *Blessed be this place, and this time,*
> *and they who are now with us.*

I think the name Dryghten best exemplifies the divine will. While the Dryghten is described by the Gardnerians in many ways, what stands out to me is "Ancient Providence." Providence, in terms of divinity, refers to the care, preparation, control, and guardianship expressed by the divine for creation. To me, this guidance and oversight are best suited to the aspect of divine will.

In the Welsh Druidic revival, the name Celi is used as the "hidden god of the heavens." Celi is the divine source of the three rays of light that manifested creation. While Celi is seen as the source, there is a masculine quality to Celi, for it is said that the Sun is the revealed presence of Celi, The feminine divine, Ced, which is perhaps a play on the name of the goddess Ceridwen, is manifested as the Earth and Venus. With this union of the divine in the term CeliCed, I see it as an expression of divine love. Love is best exemplified by the uniting power to bring things together, an expansive state of consciousness. For a Witch, the best and simplest example of this divine union is the union of Heaven and Earth, masculine and feminine, but the powers of Celi and Ced also are embodied by the Sun and Venus, and the union of Celi and Ced can be found in the astrological alignments of the Sun and Venus.

Lastly, the Scottish term Cruithear, meaning "Creator," refers to the Cruithne, or native Picts, who were seen as the "shaper people" or "created people," for they decorated themselves with the shapes of animals on their bodies. Crithear refers to the Creator, but the Creator as the Shaper. It's been considered akin to the Native concept up the Great Spirit among the Scottish Celts, but as a Shaper, the concept of Cruithear relates quite well to the Divine Mind, the part of the divine that is creative, that gives shape and form.

By calling upon the divine in its triune nature, through a deeper understanding of the will, heart, and mind, through the divine as Dryghten, CeliCed and Cruithear, individually or together, we can work more deeply with the divine as the source of the three rays. Each of our initiator paths leads to one of these divine powers. The quests of love, knowledge, and purpose each lead us to the source, and thereby unlock the mysteries of the other two facets of divinity. Look at each of these aspects of the source as the root of one of these rays while simultaneously encompassing all of creation, like the Hermeticist's concept of the Divine Mind. Yet instead of being encompassed only by the Divine Mind, we are simultaneously encompassed within the divine heart and the divine will. We are not only all thoughts within the Divine Mind, but are all love within the divine heart. We are all rays of light, of divine power, within the divine will. Only when we understand and unite all of these aspects do we have a true mystical experience of the source and can thereby return to the Garden of the Gods, creating it anew upon the Earth.

The Grand Council

With a greater understanding of the divine source and its manifestation through the levels of existence, we find a purpose and path in the scheme of creation. Our job as creatures of flesh and blood, along the crooked path, is to choose both the love of the bent path and the will of the straight path, for we are the uniting principle, having free choice. In that free choice, we learn wisdom, for the only wise choice is to truly hold both divine love and divine will. Life is an unfolding process of learning, through personal love and personal will, how to embody and hold the dual flames of divine love and divine will, opening the gate to divine wisdom through knowledge.

One of the best ways we can succeed in uniting will, love, and wisdom is by building alliances with the other races. By learning from, and in turn teaching, those of the other races incarnate through nature and excarnate through the ethers, we build bridges. We do so by forming not only passing relationships but also strong partnerships, bonds, with such entities. They aid our evolution by anchoring the energies of the ray they are most associated with in our own energy field. We aid them by holding open the bridge to the other races, so they too can expand and evolve back to the source.

When we truly bond with those of the angelic realm—aligning with divine will rather than sentimentality, which is the view many people today have the of the angels—we align with our own higher self, our Holy Guardian Angel or Watcher. When we bond with the true fey, the elder races, we align with nature and the lower self, the intuitive Shaper that is most like our child self. When we awaken our own animal nature, or bond with other animal allies and learn their medicine, their nature, we move beyond simple factual knowledge and into the realm of natural instinctive wisdom. The use of magick, through herbs, stones, and animals, attunes us to the powers of our love, will, and knowledge embodied in nature to find our divine source.

All the work of our magick, high and low, religious and mundane, leads us to the Garden of the Gods. By merging with our guides, we rekindle the consciousness from a time when all was connected, but rather than go backward, we move forward. After such separation, we can grow richer through experience and return with this richness to the collective. As we simultaneously hold love, will, and wisdom, we can simultaneously hold the paradox of individuality and unity in the Garden of the Gods.

Our collective unity can best be described as a council. In the Age of Aquarius, we turn the vertical hierarchy of the Age of Pisces on its ear, and create lateral rulership—the council, the coven, the board. While not all of us will be part of a full Grand Council, as we each tend to focus on specific types of allies based on our own personal spiritual development, theoretically any one human can be spiritually linked to any of the twelve types of entities to form a Grand Council (figure 20).

Human—The human self is what we most identify with, and even though we live in a culture that usually holds only one identity of "self," we know that we consist of at least three selves or "souls," called the Namer, Shaper, and Watcher. These three selves have to find a level of alignment before we truly can integrate with our "council." Until that time, such spirits appear solely as guides and allies. From our human perspective, we humans are the linchpin, or connecting force, between many of the allies on the council, as creatures of the third ray with free choice tend to form bridges with other realms and other races.

FIGURE 20: TWELVE-SPOKED STARRY WHEEL

Animal Totem—The animal totem relates most to the Shaper, or lower self, and is the first ally to make contact with us, because our nature is essentially animalistic. Both animals and humans are creatures of the third ray. Conscious connection to the animal ally brings protection, healing, and guidance, opening the way to further spiritual development.

Ancestor—Ancestors are those normal humans who have passed into the realm of death and commune with us. Our primary connection to the ancestors is genetic, and we most often connect to the deceased's Shaper self through the blood, though ancestral contact can be through adoption as well as spiritual bonds. We aid the spiritual evolution of those who have come before us, just as those who come after us will aid our own evolution.

Master—Members of the Mighty Dead or Hidden Company are considered to be spiritual masters, aligning the three selves and passing into a new realm of consciousness free from the requirement of reincarnation. While the ancestors forge a link to the past of humanity, the masters forge a link with us to the collective future of humanity and are ideal teachers, for they already are in the next phase of evolution, where we seek to go.

Angel—The angelic races are creatures of the first ray. They implement divine will, and council with them brings us closer to our own divine will and our own Watcher, our angelic higher self. Most magicians tend to build relationships with a particular archangel and, through that archangel, specific angelic beings from their order. The archangels we align with are most likely to have resonance with our own personal divine will.

Faery—The faery races, as creatures of the second ray, are most attuned to our lower selves and the power of nature and the land. True communion with them brings us playfulness and childlike qualities, dissolving away much of our strict polarity consciousness around social and moral absolutes, as we see more clearly through the eyes of nature.

Plant Familiar—Plant familiars, or plant totems, are plant spirit allies usually associated with one of three functions. Plants known as balms are from the realm of healing plants, bringing harmony to the body. Baneful plants hold the power of the mysteries. Trees are the elder priests/priestesses and teachers of our planetary history. A Witch can have plant familiars from all three realms, but one usually takes dominance.

Mineral Familiar—Mineral familiars, or spirits from the realm of crystals, stones, and metals, work in a manner similar to that of plant familiars. We can align with the healing and magickal powers of a particular metal or mineral and thereby align with the divine will of the deep Earth.

Land Spirit—The genius loci, or spirit of place, is the entity that embodies a particular location. Many times humans enter into a reciprocal relationship with the land where they live, and the spirit of that land. They become guardians and stewards, and in turn are brought deeper into the mysteries of the land.

Deva—Relationships with the devas, the overarching spirits of nature, are similar to those with the angels, but are usually in alignment with the forces and functions of nature and specific locations. Devas are the higher intelligences that guide nature, and attunement with them grants greater information and insight into the secrets of nature, revealing new ways of healing, building, and living. Devas also can rule over groups, institutions, and organizations. Such entities, usually co-created by humanity, are known as egregores in Western occultism. In magickal groups, these entities hold and maintain the "current" of a tradition.

Demon—As angels rule the higher impulses of the universe, demons rule the lower impulses. Though demons usually are shunned, some magicians and witches make allies out of those spirits that otherwise would be rejected. The shaman who allies with a sickness spirit, arguably a "demon," will have success curing that spirit's illness. The magick attributed to Solomon outlines a hierarchy of demons, the Goetia, that can be helpful to humanity. By working with these spirits for a higher purpose, they too evolve and move toward their own enlightenment.

God—Many priestesses and priests of the old faith focus on service to a particular deity, a patron god, who guides their work in the world. In exchange for power, knowledge, healing, and love, the Witch is the patron god's eyes, ears, voice, and hand within the world of shape and form.

Multidimensional Consciousness

Critical to attaining the state of awareness we equate with the Garden of the Gods is the ability to be multidimensional, meaning to exist consciously in many dimensions of reality at one time. Attainment of Heaven on Earth is not so much about going anywhere physically or spiritually, but simply being aware of what is already present all around you. A part of you, your Watcher, has always existed in the perfect peace of Heaven, untouched by the troubles of the world. Manifesting this heavenly existence is opening to this part of yourself consciously, not just during ritual. You must be aware of it, and exist from it at least in part, during your "normal" waking life.

One of the sacred psychic powers said to awaken in the initiate of the mysteries is the power of bi-location. Bi-location abilities can be the first introduction to this multidimensional consciousness. To bi-locate means to be at two (bi) places (locate) at once. Some believe the mighty masters of the traditions can manifest two separate and distinct bodies at two different locations. Others, myself included, believe it refers to the ability of the Double, equated with our lower Shaper self, our astral double. Our power is such that sensitive people can perceive our Double wherever it is in the world, and ultimately the double is so empowered by our consciousness that even those with underdeveloped psychic senses experience its presence as a real, living, flesh-and-blood person, even though it is simply a strong astral presence without corporeal existence.

In some faery teachings, the Double also refers to the Co-Walker, the faery ally, lover, or bride/husband that walks along with the initiate of the faery tradition. The faery spirit is said to walk along with the human, as the person's shadow. Initiates of faery traditions might say that part of the faery ally's consciousness is with us in the human world, watching through our eyes and experiencing human life, while a portion of our own consciousness has been exchanged, and is living in Faerie, looking through our ally's eyes and experiencing life in the underworld of Faerie.

In this teaching, we have a true key to multidimensional consciousness. It is not simply expanding our own consciousness to be in two or more places at once, but is the union of our consciousness with our otherworldy allies. They become multidimensional as well, aiding all our evolution and the restoration and growth of the Garden.

Initial awakening to multidimensional consciousness comes from opening the gates to higher and lower levels of consciousness. We become aware of the Underworld and Overworld and truly awaken in the Middle World. In the work of the three rays teachings, we could say the three cauldrons are turned upright, filled and activated. Each cauldron simply refers to an awakening and access to levels of consciousness usually unnoticed by the majority of people.

In more mainstream metaphysical lore, we are said to awaken and align the chakras, clearing blocks from each of the spinning energy "organs" of conscious-ness. Each chakra is like an organ within our body, but instead of processing food or air, the chakras process the life force energy of consciousness. Each one handles a different level of consciousness. At the bottom of the spectrum are more terres-trial and personal qualities of consciousness, and at the top of the spectrum are the more transpersonal aspects of consciousness. The chakras develop from more primal to more refined as we ascend the scale. None are "good" or "bad," as no color is good or bad. Every color is necessary to create the beauty of the rainbow, just as every chakra is necessary to create the beauty of human consciousness. Without the lower chakras, we cannot build a foundation to sustain the higher ones. Each is a necessary step on the path of spiritual progression. Each chakra aligns with a planet, a metal, a day of the week, and an alchemical operation in the process of creating the Elixir of Life and the Philosopher's Stone, both of which are really the quest for and culmination of enlightenment.

In the seven chakra system model, most balanced esoteric traditions urge an initiate to be grounded in the heart space, not only for its balanced and loving nature, a key to spiritual development but also because, as the heart chakra is the center of the system, one can rise or fall on the seven-note scale of consciousness more easily than when rooted higher or lower in the chakra system (figure 21).

After becoming truly rooted in the heart chakra, we engage in practices to expand our heart-centered consciousness to eventually encompass all of the chakras and the levels of consciousness they process. We expand outward from the heart, the center of love, to include both the lower solar plexus and the higher throat. Both chakras are centers of power. The solar plexus holds power and energy within our consciousness, while the throat expresses that power, speaking the words of magick to create and make changes and connections. Then the expansion continues to include the belly and brow chakras. Both of these energy centers contain knowledge, hopefully leading to wisdom. The belly chakra holds our gut level of instinctual knowledge, often regarding our safety. It is primal and defies words. The brow, or third eye, chakra holds the knowledge of the past, present, and future, containing the gifts of the Sight, the name given to the ability to look beyond the physical into otherworldly reality, including the past and future. Lastly, the consciousness expands outward to include both the root and crown chakras. Each is ultimately about survival and connection. The root chakra is survival and connection in the physical world, leaving

**FIGURE 21:
CHAKRAS WITHIN THE BODY**

us rooted in the material world and fully present in the body. Its mirror chakra, the crown, possesses the same attributes and functions, but in the spirit world. Sometimes the chakra system is described as an upside-down tree, with the roots at the top, growing into Heaven. The crown chakra keeps us present in spiritual reality and grounded in the bodies of light.

While we have peak experiences, momentary spiritual expansions that grant us a more mystical view beyond our normal daily perceptions, we cannot maintain this expanded state indefinitely. Even a disciplined, heart-centered magickal initiate with a daily practice can find it quite difficult to maintain such a state of consciousness indefinitely. Initiations, elevations, and peak experiences, both in formal traditions and in the Mystery School of Life, can confer more permanent changes on our consciousness, but it is still a challenge to maintain mystical awareness in daily life. Those with an expanded consciousness live with an inclusive worldview, understanding at least intuitively how all things are connected and part of a greater whole. The web of life connecting us all is a reality in such a state of mind, and not simply a poetic metaphor. If everybody lived at this level of awareness, we would have paradise on Earth. Sadly, such expanded consciousness is currently the exception, not the rule, in our secular societies.

Exceptional individuals can reach this level of divine awareness, but it is not the commonplace consciousness of our overall communities. We dream of enlightened, utopian societies in our mythologies, with stories of Shamballa, Shangri-La, Olmolungring, Atlantis, and Hy-Brasil, as we seek a community to support such divine awareness. Today, we have little to support us in the outer world. The support of a flesh-and-blood initiatory brotherhood and sisterhood, where the elders truly hold an expanded state of consciousness, can be a powerful ally to us. But the support of a council of spiritual elders beyond the flesh and blood can be even more powerful in our development. Ideally we should have both human and non-human support.

When we look at our spirit council as potential Co-Walkers, allies aligned with us in continual states of communion, we can more easily attain this consciousness and evolve into a new humanity, residing continuously within the Garden. We are creating within and around ourselves a gestalt entity that bridges the gap between the worlds and rays, like the lightning strike of the third ray of wisdom and the Qabalistic Tree of Life. While some fear losing their sense of individuality, I believe this fear is unfounded. This collective awareness is a true embodiment of the new aeon, starting with the Age of Aquarius. Aquarius's hallmark is the consciousness of both community and individuality. In essence, we can only truly serve our community, local and global, by being our individual and unique selves. The same is true of our union with our spiritual community beyond the flesh. We form a link with them, like the group consciousness of a tight-knit coven, lodge, or other lineage tradition, but in doing so we don't sacrifice our individuality. We elevate or expand our personal self, the Namer, merging it with the Watcher and Shaper, but essentially become more us. In this lifetime we aspire to attain what Qabalistic magicians refer to as the rank of Ipsissimus, the degree of elevation associated with the sephira of Kether. Translated as the "very very self," the Ipsissimus is your identity at the most profound level, but it is still you, holding your own divine love, will, and wisdom.

Looking Through the Eyes of the Allies

Relax your body. Relax your mind. Open your heart. Feel the divine spark within. Engage the entire self for this working and prepare yourself for spiritual communion with one of the allies you have bonded with, be it from the race of faeries, angels, or animals. You don't have to be in deep trance for this working, as ideally you later will open your eyes and move around. Close your eyes and speak this invocation:

By the straight, bent, and crooked lines,
I seek to be one with my spirit ally.
Let us walk together hand in hand, heart to heart.
Come forward now, O ally, and make your presence known to me.
Hail and welcome.

Wait until you feel the presence of an ally. If you feel comfortable with this ally, continue the exercise. Speak this incantation:

Let your thoughts become my thoughts.
And my thoughts become your thoughts.
Let your breath become my breath,
And my breath become your breath.
Let your words become my words,
Let my words become your words.
Let your eyes become my eyes,
And my eyes become your eyes.
To see truly in my world,
To see truly in your world,
To see truly in all the worlds.
So mote it be.

Feel your essence merge with that of your guide, as if you walk together in the same space at the same time. Though not the traditional Co-Walker relationship, this is a similar, albeit temporary, experience. Open your eyes.

Allow your ally to look through your eyes. Often one eye will feel more "human" and the other more spiritual. For me, the spirits usually occupy my left eye, and many right-handed people will agree, but go with what you feel is occurring in your own body. Do you see differently? If so, how? Move around and notice how the world appears different, not only visually but through all your senses and perceptions.

When you are ready, stand still. Close your eyes. Ask to look through you ally's eyes in their world. What do you perceive? For most people, this experience is very different from traditional pathworking meditations or shamanic journeys, as those experiences are processed through human consciousness, not "piggybacked" through the consciousness of another spiritual race. Allow your ally to explore their world with your consciousness looking through them.

When done, thank your ally. Prepare to release the part of yourself in the Otherworld and the part of your ally embodied in you. Say:

> *By the straight, bent, and crooked lines,*
> *I thank and release my spirit ally.*
> *Let us part with peace ever between us.*
> *Let our thoughts be our own.*
> *Let our breath be our own.*
> *Let our words be our own.*
> *Let our eyes be our own.*
> *Returned to our own worlds, our own times, and our own bodies.*
> *Blessed be.*

Bring your awareness completely back. Ground and balance yourself as needed.

While this exercise is an excellent first step in developing an expanded spirit ally consciousness, the Garden of the Gods consciousness is like holding many Co-Walker relationships at once. These relationships might not be as intense as the previous exercise in every waking moment, but developing the Garden of the Gods consciousness grants a pervading sense of sharing your perceptions and space with a multitude of entities, your Council. Each member of the Council can grant you insight into any experience, and reciprocally you can also grant insight to your allies. A true union occurs, where we become not just walkers between the worlds, but living gates between the worlds. This process of building, communing with, and enacting the living gates of our Council can take years, and even lifetimes.

Such a permanent change in consciousness is not something accomplished in a short period of time. The rituals and practices outlined here, particularly the

Garden of the Gods ritual at the end of this chapter, will facilitate a long-term shift in consciousness, allowing you to hold the expanding consciousness outside of ritual and into daily life.

The necessity of grounding—both in terms of the energetic skill to remain present and the ability to be clearly aware of the Middle World reality and all the responsibilities that go along with it—cannot be emphasized enough. To be successfully multidimensional, you must expand outward from the normal human consciousness while retaining it. You must add the expanded states of awareness to your normal human consciousness, and hold them simultaneously. Many people trade normal waking consciousness for an otherworldly meditative consciousness, leaving them ungrounded and ineffective in daily life, creating the typical flighty, daydreaming metaphysical practitioner. While such a state of consciousness is fine as a temporary state, it should not be our normal, default consciousness in which we anchor our awareness.

The beauty of humanity is our ability to bridge the dimensions and make connections, but we lose that ability if we are not rooted in the material world before we make such connections and expansions. Without a root in the material world, we go from spiritual seeker to the spiritually lost, and many prefer that rather than ever succeeding in their quest. Many people prefer to continually seek, remaining at a spiritually juvenile level of initiation, seeking only the adventure and none of the responsibilities that comes with the subsequent phases. If you become a spiritual "finder," then you begin a new and bold adventure, with different challenges and blessings, and will be of greater service to yourself, your people, and the worlds and races of both flesh and spirit.

The Garden of the Gods Ritual

The Garden of the Gods ritual assumes that you have performed all the necessary rituals and exercises in this text, and have a fundamental understanding and practice of modern Witchcraft, including casting circle, calling quarters, and creating sacred space. If you do not possess these skills, then focus on mastering them while continuing your practice with the three rays material. Then attempt the Garden of the Gods ritual.

Cleansing: Cleanse the ritual space before starting the ritual. Cleanse all participants in the ritual before entering the space. Use salt and water as well as a cleansing incense. You can use this Garden of the Gods Incense for both cleansing and to burn during the ritual.

Garden of the Gods Incense

4 parts pine needles

2 parts frankincense

2 parts myrrh

1 part cinnamon bark

1 part white oak bark

½ part mugwort

½ part patchouli

½ part yarrow flower

¼ part vervain (blue or white)

¼ part elder flower

¼ part angelica root

12 drops pine oil

12 drops frankincense oil

6 drops cinnamon oil

4 drops patchouli oil

1 part honey (to bind)

Assuming that one tablespoon equals one part, use the oil measurements given. If not, adjust accordingly. Let the incense air-dry for a few days, then bottle for a month to let the various scents mix well.

If you prefer not to make such a complex incense, then you can use one herb at a time for various parts of the ritual. The dominant scent of this blend is pine, because pine, as an herb of Jupiter, helps expand our consciousness. If you want to use only one simple incense, then you can just burn dry pine needles on self-igniting charcoal. Oak is also ruled by Jupiter and can be used with, or as a substitute for, pine. Evocation of the Middle World can be accented by patchouli, the Underworld by elder flower or myrrh, and the Upper World by angelica root or frankincense.

Main Altar: A main altar can be used for this ritual, as for any traditional rite of modern Witchcraft, though many will omit it in favor of the four quarter altars. If you choose to have a main altar, then the traditional elemental "weapons" of the pentacle, wand, chalice, and blade can be put upon it, though the only functional tool in this rite is the wand. The traditional Wiccan Great Rite with the chalice and blade shall be omitted in favor of an inner meditative cauldron working. You can have a black candle on the left of the altar for the Pillar of Severity and the Goddess, along with a white candle on the right of the altar for the Pillar of Mercy and the God. I recommend using three candles of red, yellow, and blue for the three rays, along with, or in place of, the black and white candles. If you choose not to use all five candles, then simply evoke the energies as the ritual progresses but omit the lighting of the candles. An incense thurible for charcoal is needed if you use the handmade Garden of the Gods Incense recipe provided here. Decorate the remaining portions of the altar with any items that connect you to the angels, faeries, animals, plants, and minerals.

Casting the Circle: Using one of your three ray wands, or any wooden wand you feel is appropriate, cast the circle three times deosil. Envision one ring in ruby red light for the heavens. Envision the second ring in fiery blue flame for the Underworld. Envision the third ring in golden yellow light for the Middle World. Say:

We cast the crimson seeds of this circle hedge and charge them to go forth and bloom toward the heavens in flower and thorn, protecting us from all that may come to do harm.

We nourish the hedge with the azure blessings of faery flame, to grow roots deep and strong into the depths of the Underworld.

We bind this circle hedge in the golden lightning of Witchfire, to guard us in the heavens, Earth, and Underworld, to usher in the Garden of the Gods where divine will, love, and wisdom are sovereign. So mote it be.

Invocation to the Three Rays: Summon forth the three primal powers from the source into the circle:

By the straight line,
We invoke the first ray,
We invoke the red ray.
We invoke the unbending ray of cold red archangelic flame.
We invoke the ray of will and power.

By the bent line,
We invoke the second ray.
We invoke the blue ray.
We invoke the spiraling ray of electric blue faery flame.
We invoke the ray of love and trust.

By the crooked line,
We invoke the third ray.
We invoke the yellow ray.
We invoke the crooked ray of serpentine gold Witch fire.
We invoke the ray of wisdom and cunning.

Calling the Quarters: Open the four elemental gates in the three worlds, starting with the Middle World, then the Underworld, and lastly the Upper World.

Have four small altars in the four quarters. As each altar can embody more than one element, you do not have to have the decorations or altar cloth match one specific element, but use materials you feel are in harmony with the overall direction for the ritual. Here are some suggestions for what to put on each altar (chart 20):

Direction	Colors	Items
North	Black, blue, yellow, brown	Snake fetish, mandrake, bowl of water, yellow candle, lemon essential oil, angelite
East	Yellow, brown, green	Bat fetish, monkshood, bowl of water, green candle, patchouli essential oil, emerald
South	Red, yellow	Wolf fetish, henbane, bowl of water, red candle, cinnamon essential oil, ruby
West	Blue, green	Frog fetish, datura, bowl of water, blue candle, rose essential oil, aquamarine

CHART 20: TOOLS OF THE FOUR DIRECTIONS

Fetishes can be simply any representation of the animal, such as a picture, a carving, or other symbol of the animal. Fetishes are used in shamanic forms of magick to both represent and form a link with the animal spirit totem.

The plant material can be in the form of a tincture, tea, flower essence, or powdered herb. These banes can be difficult to obtain, so if you decide to change your plant allies, choose those plants spirits whose herbs are easier to obtain at shops and apothecaries. Those who have more experience with plant banes probably will grow their own, though mandrake is still the most difficult to get. You can substitute the American mandrake, or May apple, or even better yet the homeopathic remedy of mandrake. Just a small pinch or a few drops in a clear bowl of spring water is a powerful anchor for the presence of these spirits in our circle. The ideal would be to perform the ritual in a garden where all the plant spirits called are currently growing.

For the heavenly quarters, candles are one of the best ways of aligning with the fire of the stars. Each candle is colored according to the appropriate heavenly element and carved with the glyph of the corresponding zodiac sign:

Aquarius-air-yellow, Taurus-earth-green, Leo-fire-red, Scorpio-water-blue (figure 22). You can anoint the candle with essential oils. Generally, essential oils are cut with a base oil, with 5 to 7 drops of essential oil to ⅛ ounce of base oil such as grapeseed, apricot kernel, or jojoba oil. Candles should be anointed from the top down to the base, to symbolize drawing in the power of the heavens to your sacred space. The stones are an additional link connecting heavenly will with the Earth and the Underworld, for they hold divine will in the heart of the planet.

Calling the Four Powers of the Middle World

Face north and evoke the power of elemental earth. If possible, hold up a Snake fetish or emblem when calling the power of earth.

> *To the north,*
> *We call to the element of earth in the Great Between.*
> *We call to the spirit of Snake, ever changing, shedding her skin.*
> *Snake, the keeper of kundalini,*
> *Awaken the Witch power within us.*
> *Hail and welcome.*

Face east and evoke the power of elemental air. If possible, hold up a Bat fetish or emblem when calling the power of air.

FIGURE 22: GLYPHS OF AQUARIUS, TAURUS, LEO, AND SCORPIO

To the east,
We call upon the element of air in the Great Between.
We call to the spirit of Bat, blind guide, flying by night.
Bat, the navigator of night,
Awaken the Witch eye within us.
Hail and welcome.

Face south and evoke the power of elemental fire. If possible, hold up a Wolf fetish or emblem when calling the power of fire.

To the south,
We call to the element of fire in the Great Between.
We call to the spirit of Wolf, teacher and protector, guiding the pack.
Wolf, the hunter of instinct,
Awaken the Witch soul within us.
Hail and welcome.

Face west and evoke the power of elemental water. If possible, hold up a Frog fetish or emblem when calling the power of water.

To the west,
We call upon the element of water in the Great Between.
We call upon the spirit of Frog, transformer, water to land.
Frog, the singer of song,
Awaken the Witch heart within us.
Hail and welcome.

Calling the Four Powers of the Underworld

Face north and evoke the power of elemental earth. Place a small amount of mandrake in the bowl of water. Stamp your foot three times upon the ground after the evocation but before speaking "Hail and welcome."

To the north,
We call to the element of earth in the Great Below,
and we call to the green spirits of wisdom.
We call the bane Mandrake, root of love, death, and wisdom.
Mandragora of the midnight scream that brings madness,

Whisper the secrets of the deep earth to us.
Hail and welcome.

Face east and evoke the power of elemental fire. Place a small amount of monkshood in the bowl of water. Stamp your foot three times upon the ground after the evocation but before speaking "Hail and welcome."

To the east,
We call to the element of fire in the Great Below,
And we call to the green spirits of power.
We call to the bane Monkshood, bane of wolves and slayer of monsters,
Aconite of the hooded veil, burning angel of death.
Hail and welcome.

Face south and evoke the power of elemental air. Place a small amount of henbane in the bowl of water. Stamp your foot three times upon the ground after the evocation but before speaking "Hail and welcome."

To the south,
We call to the element of air in the Great Below,
and we call to the green spirits of knowledge.
We call to the bane of Devil's-eye, Henbane, giver of second sight, true sight,
Black Solanaceae, summoner of storms and winds of whispering knowledge.
Hail and welcome.

Face west and evoke the power of elemental water. Place a small amount of datura in the bowl of water. Stamp your foot three times upon the ground after the evocation but before speaking "Hail and welcome."

To the west,
We call to the element of water in the Great Below,
and we call to the green spirits of love.
We call to the bane of Thorn Apple, the angel trumpet.
Datura, open the heart and soul with your venom and numb us from
*   overwhelming pain.*
Hail and welcome.

Calling of the Four Powers of the Upper World

Face north and evoke the power of elemental air. Anoint the yellow candle carved with the symbol of Aquarius with lemon essential oil. Hold the angelite stone above your head with both hands as you evoke the element.

To the north,
We call to the element of air in the Great Above.
We open the northern gate of the Water Bearer.
We seek the ancient watcher in the eye of Aquarius, Fomalhaut,
And the archangel of air, Raphael, the divine physician.
Awaken us to the ways of healing and guard us in this rite.
Hail and welcome.

Face east and evoke the power of elemental earth. Anoint the green candle carved with the symbol of Taurus with patchouli essential oil. Hold the emerald stone above your head with both hands as you evoke the element.

To the east,
We call to the element of earth in the Great Above.
We open the eastern gate of the Bull.
We seek the ancient watcher in the eye of Taurus, Aldebaran,
And the archangel of earth, Uriel, keeper of secret knowledge.
Awaken us to the mysteries of nature and guard us in this rite.
Hail and welcome.

Face south and evoke the power of elemental fire. Anoint the red candle carved with the symbol of Leo with cinnamon essential oil. Hold the ruby stone above your head with both hands as you evoke the element.

To the south,
We call to the element of fire in the Great Above.
We open the southern gate of the Lion.
We seek the ancient watcher in the heart of Leo, Regulus,
And the archangel of fire, Michael, heavenly protector.
Awaken us to the power of the warrior and guard us in this rite.
Hail and welcome.

Face west and evoke the power of elemental water. Anoint the blue candle carved with the symbol of Scorpio with rose essential oil. Hold the aquamarine stone above your head with both hands as you evoke the element.

To the west,
We call to the element of water in the Great Above.
We open the western gate of the Scorpion.
We seek the ancient watcher in the heart of Scorpio, Antares,
And the archangel of water, Gabriel, messenger of the heart.
Awaken us to the blessings of the cup and guard us in this rite.
Hail and welcome.

Calling the Powers

We call forth the power of the divine will.
We call to the heavenly angelic races of True Purpose.
Please be present in our rite.

Light the red candle on the left of the altar.

We call forth the love of the divine heart.
We call to the chthonic faery races of Perfect Love.
Please be present in our rite.

Light the blue candle on the right of the altar.

We call forth the wisdom of the Divine Mind.
We call to the flesh and blood races of Perfect Trust.
Please be present in our rite.

Light the yellow candle between the red and blue candles.

We call forth those who have united will, love, and wisdom within.
We call to the Goddesses and Gods.

Light the black and white candles.

We call to the Mighty Dead, Hidden Company of Witches,
The Timeless Order of the Nameless Art.
We call to all spirits who come in Perfect Love and Perfect Trust,

In complete alignment with our purpose.
Please make your presence known.
Hail and welcome.

Sacrament of Awen: Rather than unite the Goddess and God through the Ritual of the Great Rite with a sacramental chalice of wine and ritual athame, unite the three rays within the three cauldrons. You can repeat the Third Cauldron Working in chapter 4. Here is a shortened, ritualized form of it.

Call down the first ray:

By the straight line,
I invoke the first ray.
I invoke the red ray.
I invoke the unbending ray of cold red archangelic flame.
I invoke the ray of will and power.
What is the will of the heavens?

Listen. Feel.
I enact the will of the heavens.
Draw the red ray down into the head.
What is the will of the head?
Listen. Feel.
I enact the will of the head.
Draw the red ray down into the heart, which now turns into golden flame.
What is the will of the heart?
Listen. Feel.
I enact the will of the heart.
Drawn the red ray down into the belly, which now burns with white flame.
What is the will of the body?
Listen. Feel.
I enact the will of the body.
Drawn the red ray down into the Underworld.
What is the will of the Earth and Underworld?
Listen. Feel.
I enact the will of the Earth and Underworld.
There are no limits to my power. All is possible.

Call down the second ray:

By the bent line,
I invoke the second ray.
I invoke the blue bay.
I invoke the spiraling ray of electric blue faery flame.
I invoke the ray of love and trust.
What is the love of the heavens?
Listen. Feel.
I enact the love of the heavens.
Draw the blue ray down into the head.
What is the love of the head?
Listen. Feel.
I feel the love of the head.
Draw the blue ray down into the heart, which now turns into green flame.
What is the love of the heart?
Listen. Feel.
I feel the love of the heart.
Drawn the blue ray down into the belly, which now burns with black flame.
What is the love of the body?
Listen. Feel.
I feel the love of the body.
Drawn the blue ray down into the Underworld.
What is the love of the Earth and Underworld?
Listen. Feel.
I feel the love of the Earth and Underworld.
There are no limits to my love. All is one.

Call down the third ray:

By the crooked line,
I invoke the third ray.
I invoke the yellow ray.
I invoke the crooked ray of serpentine gold Witch fire.
What is the wisdom of the heavens?
Listen. Feel.
I know the wisdom of the heavens.
Draw the yellow ray down into the head.
What is the wisdom of the head?

Listen. Feel.

I know the wisdom of the head.

Draw the yellow ray down into the heart, which now turns into red flame.

What is the wisdom of the heart?

Listen. Feel.

I know the wisdom of the heart.

Drawn the yellow ray down into the belly, which now burns with scarlet flame.

What is the wisdom of the body?

Listen. Feel.

I know the wisdom of the body.

Drawn the yellow ray down into the Underworld.

What is the wisdom of the Earth and Underworld?

Listen. Feel.

I know the wisdom of the Earth and Underworld.

There are no limits to my wisdom. All is known.

Vision of the Garden of the Gods: Open yourself to the vision of the Garden of the Gods. In this sacred space, the heavens, land, and Underworld intersect, and the three primary races mingle in perfect harmony. If you are doing this ritual in a group, and were not specifically a quarter caller previously in the ritual, then pick one of the twelve gates with its element and entity and focus on it. If you are a quarter caller, then focus on the element and entity you called upon. Which world, element, and race do you have the strongest link with? Start there. If you don't feel a specific connection to any of the twelve guardians, then evoke your own personal ally into the Garden.

Envision yourself in the Garden with your ally. Reach out to allies in the other two worlds with whom you feel less of a connection. Try to unite your consciousness, expanding it beyond your comfortable realm into all three realms simultaneously as you stand in the Garden of the Gods. With your three cauldrons filled with the three rays, find your three selves come into alignment. You are the Namer, Shaper, and Watcher simultaneously, the Three in One. You can imagine yourself as one of the other great race of bridging priests and priestesses, the Tree Teachers, with your energetic "branches" in the heavens and your "roots" in the depths of the Underworld, yet you can still move and walk.

Journey into the Garden with a Shamanic Drum: Ideally the ritual drummer will divide the journey into three drum patterns. The first is for the Underworld. Journey into the Underworld with all your allies. The second is for the Upper

World. Go through the heart of the Underworld until you reach the stars with your allies. The third beat pattern is for the Middle World. Bring all of your allies back to the Great Between, the center. Return to the Middle World, opening your eyes but without losing your magickal sight. See the world, the temple, and your fellow participants in their divine glory, standing in the primal vision of creation, expanded in consciousness through the three worlds. Walk the "garden" space of the ritual, and embrace your fellow gardeners with the words of Aleister Crowley's Gnostic Mass modified for this ritual:

There is no part of you that is not of the Gods.

Working for the Alignment of the Earth: The final act of magick in the Garden is to spread its seeds out into the world so many gardens will spring forth. Eventually we seek to spiritually re-seed the world with the fertile spiritual power of the Garden, so our entire planet will return to the Garden. Everybody will return in their own way, through their own paradigm, but a sense of connection and attunement among all things will be established. The vision is so universal that we can each experience the Garden in our own religious paradigm.

The energy for the working is generated through ecstatic community dance. Ideally, there are enough participants to form three circles of hand-holding dance. If not, then form only one. The inner ring of dancers face outward from the center and move widdershins, holding hands and moving in a grapevine step. They embody the energies of the Underworld and the faery and plant realms. The middle ring of dancers each put their left hand on the left shoulder of the person in front of them, moving deosil in a circle, with their right hand stretched outward toward the third ring. This middle ring embodies the Middle World and the races of flesh and blood, including humanity. From the edges of their vision they can see from both the inner and outer rings, connecting them. The third ring of dancers face inward toward the center of the circle. They, too, are holding hands and moving widdershins in a grapevine step. They embody the heavens, stars, and angelic races.

The Dance

The ritual drummer starts with a slow and steady beat, gradually increasing the tempo until the dance builds to a frenzy. On the signal from the ritual leader, handholding is broken and everybody raises the Cone of Power, creating a vortex of energy by lifting their hands upward with the intention of releasing the energy as the spell is recited:

In the name of the three rays,
In the name of the three races,
In the name of all the gods and goddesses,
We cast the seeds of the Garden out,
To take root and stalk,
To grow leaf and bud, flower and fruit,
To open the gates and renew the original vision of creation,
Where all is in harmony with the heavens, Earth, and Underworld,
As it was, as it is, as it always shall be.
So mote it be.

Grounding: Ground after the release of the Cone of Power in any way you are guided to do so, in any way that is correct and good for you. Rather than completely returning your awareness to "normal" consciousness, try to "ground" your awareness both "up" and "down" the consciousness spectrum, through both your roots and branches. Our goal is to return from the ritual in alignment with the consciousness of the primordial Garden within us, and to model that for the rest of the world. Though we shall say farewell to our allies who must go, many of us will retain our connection to them as we leave the space and go into the waking world.

Devocation of the Gods and Hidden Company: Release the entities from this space, but petition them to continue their regular communion with you. If you lit any working candles on the main altar, extinguish them now. Say:

We thank the power of the divine will and the angelic races.
We thank the power of the divine love and the faery races.
We thank the power of the Divine Mind and the flesh and blood races.
We thank the goddesses and gods of Heaven, Earth, and the Underworld.
We thank the Hidden Company of our Timeless and Nameless Order.
We thank all spirits who come in Perfect Love and Perfect Trust.
May we stay in continual communion for our highest good, harming none,
Carrying out the Garden of the Gods into creation, planting seeds in all the
*   realms and all the races.*
So mote it be.

Release of the Quarters: Close the four elemental gateways just as you opened them. Reverse your working, always starting in the north, but moving widdershins from the Upper World to the Underworld and Middle World.

Release of the Four Quarters in the Upper World

Face north and devoke the power of elemental air. Extinguish the yellow candle.

> *To the north of the Great Above,*
> *We thank and release the element of air.*
> *We close the northern gate of the Water Bearer,*
> *And say farewell to the watching star Fomalhaut and the archangel Raphael.*
> *Hail and farewell.*

Face west and devoke the power of elemental water. Extinguish the blue candle.

> *To the west of the Great Above,*
> *We thank and release the element of water.*
> *We close the western gate of the Scorpion,*
> *And say farewell to the watching star Antares and the archangel Gabriel.*
> *Hail and farewell.*

Face south and devoke the power of elemental fire. Extinguish the red candle.

> *To the south of the Great Above,*
> *We thank and release the element of fire.*
> *We close the southern gate of the Lion,*
> *And say farewell to the watching star Regulus and the archangel Michael.*
> *Hail and farewell.*

Face east and devoke the power of elemental earth. Extinguish the green candle.

> *To the east of the Great Above,*
> *We thank and release the element of earth.*
> *We close the eastern gate of the Bull,*
> *And say farewell to the watching star Aldebaran and the archangel Uriel.*
> *Hail and farewell.*

Release of the Four Quarters in the Underworld

Face north and devoke the power of elemental earth. If outdoors, pour the mandrake herbal water out upon the land.

> *To the north of the Great Below,*
> *We thank and release the element of earth and the green spirits of wisdom.*

We thank and release the bane of Mandrake, human root of wisdom.
Hail and farewell.

Face west and devoke the power of elemental water. If outdoors, pour the datura herbal water out upon the land.

To the west of the Great Below,
We thank and release the element of water and the green spirits of love.
We thank and release the bane of Thorn Apple, the angel trumpet.
Hail and farewell.

Face south and devoke the power of elemental air. If outdoors, pour the henbane herbal water out upon the land.

To the south in the Great Below,
We thank and release the element of air and the green spirits of knowledge.
We thank and release the bane of Henbane, giver of second sight.
Hail and farewell.

Face east and devoke the power of elemental fire. If outdoors, pour the monkshood herbal water out upon the land.

To the east of the Great Below,
We thank and release the element of fire and the green spirits of power.
We thank and release the bane of Monkshood, burning angel of death.
Hail and farewell.

Release of the Four Quarters in the Middle World

Face north and devoke the power of elemental earth. If possible, hold up a Snake fetish or emblem when releasing the power of earth.

To the north of the Great Between,
We thank and release the element of earth and the spirit of Snake.
Thank you for awakening the Witch power.
Hail and farewell.

Face west and devoke the power of elemental water. If possible, hold up a Frog fetish or emblem when releasing the power of water.

To the west of the Great Between,
We thank and release the element of water and the spirit of Frog.
Thank you for awakening the Witch heart.
Hail and farewell.

Face south and devoke the power of elemental fire. If possible, hold up a Wolf fetish or emblem when releasing the power of fire.

To the south of the Great Between,
We thank and release the element of fire and the spirit of Wolf.
Thank you for awakening the Witch soul.
Hail and farewell.

Face east and devoke the power of elemental air. If possible, hold up a Bat fetish or emblem when releasing the power of air.

To the east of the Great Between,
We thank and release the element of air and the spirit of Bat.
Thank you for awakening the Witch eye.
Hail and farewell.

Release the Three Rays: Release the three primal powers from the source to continue their journey throughout creation.

By a straight line,
By a bent line,
By a crooked line,
There are no limits to our power. All is possible.
There are no limits to our love. All is one.
There are no limits to our wisdom. All is known.
We release the rays of power, love, and wisdom from this space.
May you travel forth and become one within us.

Release the Circle: Using the wand that cast the circle, move widdershins around the ritual space, sending out the circle infinitely across the cosmos.

We cast the petals and seeds of this circle out into the cosmos to plant the Garden of the Gods all across creation. As it was, as it is, as it ever shall be. So mote it be.

BIBLIOGRAPHY

Bailey, Alice A. *The Rays and the Initiations.* New York: Lucis Publishing, 1960.

Blavatsky, Helena P. *Isis Unveiled.* Wheaton, IL: Theosophical Publishing House, 1972.
———. *The Secret Doctrine.* Adyar, India: Theosophical Publishing House, 1888.

Case, Paul Foster. *Esoteric Keys of Alchemy.* 1932; reprint, Burnaby, British Columbia, Canada: Ishtar Publishing, 2006.

Davidson, Gustav. *A Dictionary of Angels, Including the Fallen Angels.* New York: Free Press, 1967.

Fortune, Dion. *Esoteric Orders and Their Work.* Foreword by Gareth Knight. York Beach, ME: Samuel Weiser, 2000.
———. *The Mystical Qabalah.* York Beach, ME: Samuel Weiser, 2000.

———. *The Sea Priestess.* York Beach, ME: Samuel Weiser, 1972.
Goddard, David. *The Sacred Magic of the Angels.* York Beach, ME: Samuel Weiser, 1996.

Greer, John Michael. *Circles of Power.* St. Paul, MN: Llewellyn Publications, 2002.
———. *The Druidry Handbook: Spiritual Practice Rooted in the Living Earth.* York Beach, ME: Red Wheel/Weiser, 2006.
———. *The New Encyclopedia of the Occult.* St. Paul, MN: Llewellyn Publications, 2003.

Grimassi, Raven. *The Witches' Craft.* St. Paul, MN: Llewellyn Publications, 2002.
———. *The Witch's Familiar.* St. Paul, MN: Llewellyn Publications, 2003.

Grimassi, Raven, and Stephanie Taylor. *The Seeker's Guide to the Hidden Path.* Woodbury, MN: Llewellyn Publications, 2007.
———. *A Traveler's Guide to the Well Worn Path.* St. Paul, MN: Llewellyn Publications, 2005.

Guiley, Rosemary Ellen. *The Encyclopedia of Witches and Witchcraft.* New York: Checkmark Books, 1999.

Harris, Mike. *Awen: The Quest of the Celtic Mysteries.* Foreword by Gareth Knight. Oceanside, CA: Sun Chalice Books, 1999.

Hauck, Dennis William. *Alchemy: Alchemistic Philosophy, Module One*. Sacramento, CA: ETX Seminars, 1999.

Herne, Richard. *Magick, Shamanism & Taoism: The I Ching in Ritual and Meditation*. St. Paul, MN: Llewellyn Publications, 2001.

Laurie, Erynn Rowan. 1996. *The Cauldron of Poesy*. Madstone Press. http://www.thunderpaw.com/neocelt/poesy.htm (accessed May 2010).

Manwaring, Kevan. *The Bardic Handbook*. Glastonbury, England: Gothic Images Publications, 2006.

Matthews, Caitlin and John. *Encyclopedia of Celtic Wisdom*. New York: Barnes & Noble, 1996.

Merry, Eleanor C. *The Flaming Door: The Mission of the Celtic Folk-Soul*. London: Rider and Company, 1936.

Sams, Jamie, and David Carson. *Medicine Cards: The Discovery of Power Through the Ways of Animals*. Santa Fe, New Mexico: Bear and Company, 1998.

Stewart, R. J. *The Merlin Tarot*. Element Books, Ltd., 2002.
———. *Robert Kirk: Walker Between the Worlds: A New Edition of the The Secret Commonwealth of Elves, Fauns & Fairies*. Roanoke, VA: R. J. Stewart Books, 2007.
———. *The Sphere of Art*. Arcata, CA: R. J. Stewart Books, 2008.

INDEX

A

Abred 29, 34

air 21, 57, 65, 67, 68, 90, 117, 118, 140, 141, 154, 178, 184, 187, 188, 189, 190, 197, 198, 199

alchemy 22, 51, 57, 58, 63, 102, 109, 200, 201

Aldebaran 142, 143, 145, 168, 190, 197

ancestor 77, 132

animal 49, 77, 88, 91, 92, 116, 117, 118, 119, 120, 121, 124, 125, 134, 140, 141, 166, 167, 169, 174, 175, 186

Annwn 27, 29, 32, 33, 34, 67, 130

Antares 168, 191, 197

Aquarius 22, 168, 174, 180, 187, 190

archfey 86, 87, 111, 158

Arthur 97, 148, 161

Asgard 29, 30

ash 28, 29, 47, 113, 131, 132, 133, 134, 136, 140, 142

Atlantis 11, 35, 42, 91, 165, 180

Avagddu 19

Avalon 29, 140, 165

awen 14, 19, 20, 21, 25, 27, 29, 34, 44, 45, 46, 47, 48, 50, 62, 64, 66, 91

B

Bailey, Alice 11, 42, 200

bile 28, 48

C

Blavatsky, H.P. 10, 42, 200

blessing 51, 102, 104, 172

blood 36, 49, 64, 84, 86, 88, 96, 104, 114, 115, 117, 119, 121, 130, 133, 134, 137, 140, 141, 148, 151, 152, 153, 154, 155, 156, 157, 158, 159, 173, 175, 178, 180, 191, 195, 196

Bodhi 28

Bowers, Roy 13

Brahman 22, 23, 39

C

Cabot, Laurie 12

Cauldron 2, 14, 25, 49, 51, 57, 60, 61, 62, 64, 65, 66, 67, 68, 69, 70, 72, 73, 74, 130, 131, 134, 192, 201

Cauldron of Poesy 57, 60, 61, 201

CeliCed 145, 171, 172, 173

Ceridwen 19, 20, 24, 172

Ceugant 29, 34

chakra 59, 61, 64, 66, 118, 178, 179, 180

chohan 43, 44

cingulum 123

Cochrane, Robert 13, 14, 157

Creirwy 19

Crowley, Aleister 12, 103, 156, 165, 195

Crowther, Patricia 172

Cruithear 145, 171, 173

cursing 51, 102, 104, 111, 112, 137

ABOUT THE AUTHOR

Christopher Penczak is an award winning author, teacher and healing practitioner. As an advocate for the timeless perennial wisdom of the ages, he is rooted firmly in the traditions of modern witchcraft and Earth based religions, but draws from a wide range of spiritual traditions including shamanism, alchemy, herbalism, Theosophy and Hermetic Qabalah to forge his own magickal traditions. His many books include *Magick of Reiki, Spirit Allies, The Mystic Foundation* and *The Inner Temple of Witchcraft.* He is the co-founder of the Temple of Witchcraft tradition and not for profit religious organization to advance the spiritual traditions of witchcraft, as well as the co-founder of Copper Cauldron Publishing, a company dedicated to producing books, recordings and tools for magickal inspiration and evolution. He has been a faculty member of the North Eastern Institute of Whole Health and a founding member of The Gifts of Grace, an interfaith foundation dedicated to acts of community service, both based in New Hampshire. He maintains a teaching and healing practice in New England, but travels extensively lecturing. More information can be found at *www.christopherpenczak.com* and *www.templeofwitchcraft.org.*

THE TEMPLE
OF WITCHCRAFT:
MYSTERY SCHOOL AND SEMINARY

Witchcraft is a tradition of experience, and the best way to experience the path of the Witch is to actively train in its magickal and spiritual lessons. The Temple of Witchcraft provides a complete system of training and tradition, with four degrees found in the Mystery School for personal and magickal development and a final fifth degree in the Seminary for the training of High Priestesses and High Priests interested in serving the gods, spirits, and community as ministers. Teachings are divided by degree into the Oracular, Fertility, Ecstatic, Gnostic, and Resurrection Mysteries. Training emphasizes the ability to look within, awaken your own gifts and abilities, and perform both lesser and greater magicks for your own evolution and the betterment of the world around you.

The Temple of Witchcraft offers both in-person and online courses with direct teaching and mentorship. Classes use the *Temple of Witchcraft* series of books and CD Companions as primary texts, supplemented monthly with information from the Temple's Book of Shadows, MP3 recordings of lectures and meditations from our founders, social support through group discussion with classmates, and direct individual feedback from a mentor.

For more information and current schedules, please visit *www.templeofwitchcraft.org*.

LaVergne, TN USA
13 December 2010
208423LV00003B/38/P